THE CRIME OF SILENCE

ORISON SWETT MARDEN

COPYRIGHT 2018
Premium Classic Books

Premiumclassicbooks@gmail.com

CONTENTS

TO THOSE WHO DO NOT KNOW 2
PREFACE 3
 1 5
PURITY IS POWER 5
 2 13
THE CRIME OF SILENCE 13
 3 27
"DANGEROUS PASSING" 27
 4 33
"A LITTLE DEYIL TO PLAY WITH" 33
 5 41
WHITE SLAVERY AND THE CHILD WOMAN 41
 6 49
HOW THE SLAVE MART IS SUPPLIED 49
 7 57
SMUGGLING POISONED GOODS 57
 8 65
MOTHERS AND DAUGHTERS 65
 9 73
PERILOUS *PLEASURES* 73
 10 80
FATHERS AND SONS 80
 11 90
SOWING WILD OATS AND THE HARVEST 90
 12 101
MEDICAL QUACKS AND "LOST MANHOOD" 101
 13 110
HOW. TO REGAIN YOUR MANHOOD 110
 14 120
WHY THE 'UNFORTUNATE WOMAN' 120
 15 131

PERILS OF THE NEW FREEDOM..131

16.. 136
WOMAN'S CRUELTY TO WOMAN 136

17.. 145
THE DAMNABLE DOUBLE STANDARD 145

ABOUT THIS BOOK

The Crime of Silence is very different from other Marden's books. It is cry to an ultra-conservative society (on the surface), to deal with the issues and problems from sexuality, and the lack of education in this subject in the beginning of last century. It is also a call to parents to talk to their sons and daughters about sexuality, to protect them from a world ready to take advantage of their ignorance.

TO THOSE WHO DO NOT KNOW

The multitudes of young men and young women who are ignorant of the perils to which their lack of sex training may expose them; the victims of wild oats sowing who are now reaping the frightful harvest in untold mental and physical agonies as a result of such ignorance; the millions of fathers and mothers whose criminal silence on this most important of all subjects may ruin the lives of the sons and daughters for whose happiness they would make any sacrifice; to my unknown friends scattered all over the world whom I have never met, but who, I feel, are one with me in the desire to give the world a lift for the things worthwhile, this little book is affectionately dedicated by The Author

PREFACE

How shall we teach sex hygiene? How shall we safeguard our children from possible sex perversion or contamination? How shall we best forewarn and forearm them so that they may transmit the family blood without contamination or impurity, may pass the family name down to their children as pure as they received it?

Never before were those questions uppermost in the minds of so many fathers, mothers, preachers, teachers and people of all classes as to-day.

We are slowly awakening to their tremendous import. The age-old crime of silence in regard to sex matters is at last being broken. In the light of modern progressive thought it seems incomprehensible that society should so long have conspired to pass over in silence this vital subject, thus, year after year, exposing millions of our youths to the frightful dangers flowing from ignorance of it. Probably the statement of a recent physician writer in this connection is not exaggerated. "Pick out any ten men you meet in the street," he says, "and at least nine will be suffering from some sort of present or past immorality."

All the wars of history have not caused anything like the number of tragedies which have been caused by this criminal silence. There is nothing so much needed to-day as non-prurient, scientific sexual instruction.

"If you have been upon these waters twenty-five years," said a young man to the captain of a steamer, "you must know every rock and sandbank in the river." "No, I don't," was the reply, "but I know where the deep water is."

It is not so much the object of the author of this book to make a chart of the dangers to be avoided in life's voyage as to mark out a course that is sane and safe.

It is sent forth as a beacon, in the hope that it will be the means of guiding voyagers away from the sex rocks and reefs on which unnumbered youths have been wrecked in the past because they were not safeguarded by the light of self-knowledge.

1

PURITY IS POWER

My strength is as the strength of ten. Because my heart is pure.— Alfred Tennyson.

Virtue could see to do what Virtue would
By her own radiant light, though sun and moon
Were in the flat sea sunk.— John Milton.

A LEADING lawyer and public official in the Sandwich Islands overturned a lighted lamp on his hand and was amazed to find that the blazing oil caused no pain. On examination he was horrified to discover that he was a leper.

In its early stages moral leprosy causes no physical pain. On the contrary, its insidious-ness lies in the very fact that it gives its victim gross, sensual pleasure. While titillating the lower animal nature, it gradually tends to numb the spiritual, to blot out the image of the Divine in man. As opium deadens the physical sensibilities, so sexual impurity, while treacherously undermining the body, deadens the moral sensibilities, and soothes the wrongdoer into unconsciousness of his peril.

There is a profound philosophy in the lines which Tennyson puts into the mouth of the stainless young knight, Sir Galahad,—

My strength is as the strength of ten. Because my heart is pure.

Purity strengthens; impurity weakens. One is constructive; the other is destructive. Purity builds up; impurity tears down.

Purity is power because it means integrity of thought, integrity of conduct. It means wholeness. The impure man cannot be a great power because he cannot thoroughly believe in himself when conscious that he is rotten in any part of his nature. Impurity works like a leaven: it affects everything in a man. The very consciousness that impurity is working within him robs him of power. He may prosper for a time, but there is a canker at work in his nature which ultimately destroys him.

In every realm of life,—the physical, moral, mental, intellectual,—there is no more practical, necessary, health-preserving, success-assuring command than "Keex3 thyself pure." It is the youth's greatest commandment. Do not listen to those who tell you that "vice is a necessity." Nothing is a necessity that is wrong. All wickedness is weakness. Vice and vigor have nothing whatever in common. Purity is strength, health, power, character. It is the divinity in man. "Blessed are the pure in heart for they shall see God" should have been translated "for they do see God."

It is only the pure in heart who can see God, or the divine in man. "A pure heart is the end of all religion, and the beginning of divinity." Impurity, on the other hand, forms a scale upon our eyes, covers the spiritual vision with a curtain, blinding us to all that is pure, clean and lovely. It draws a veil between man and his Creator. It shuts the door between its victim and his God, so that he no longer sees or appreciates divine qualities.

Purity of life means, for man no less than for woman, physical and moral health. It means efficiency, harmony of faculties, increased self-confidence. It means courage as against cowardice, a positive as against a negative mind. It means initiative, force, instead of imitation, dependence.

No one not familiar with the facts knows the fearful mental effects of the violation and abuse of the sex function. There is no other thing that so affects the mind as the consciousness that there is something wrong with the sex life. Thousands of people have committed suicide because of the mental depression caused by the consciousness of contracting a sexual disease which they thought incurable. A young man once came to me for advice with a revolver in his pocket, and told me that unless I could give him encouragement or tell him where he could get relief he would end it all then and there.

Everything in the human organism shows that purity, cleanliness and right living in every form are not only entirely normal and natural, but are absolutely imperative to human integrity, for everywhere that sexual impurity has been introduced into society, a terrible curse has followed. Demoralization, deterioration, tragedy and death of all that is highest and noblest in humanity are its legitimate fruits. Immorality, impurity, always and everywhere blights, blasts, deadens. It is the great curse of the race.

On the other hand, to be superbly sexed, without hereditary taint or acquired sex abuse or misuse, means more than anything else to the individual. Nothing else will contribute so much to mental virility, to creative power of the brain, as consciousness of sexual integrity and sexual virility, which awakens, enriches, and vitalizes all the faculties, and develops the creative energy which renews the whole nature.

It is the law that any human function whose normal, direct exercise is for any reason denied will be transmuted through other channels into general life force. This creative force, which most people squander and wickedly waste in beastly indulgences, in the virtuous man is transmuted into brain power, soul power. It is the very flowering out of life. (Men who lead a pure, clean life are infinitely more virile, more magnetic, more forceful, more productive, more buoyant, more spiritual than those who squander their creative energy and waste their vitality in dissipation.

Purity means virility and is the very spirit of the master book, the master painting, the master creation, in every department of human activity. It is this sex virility which does the most superb thing in every line of human endeavor. It is this that sparkles in the life. It is the secret of spontaneity, of buoyancy. It is the very soul of joy and gladness. Intellectual integrity is impossible without moral integrity. If there is any disintegration or demoralizing influence operating anywhere in the nature, weakness is inevitable. No one can live a life which is sapping his vitality, which is running counter to the highest thing in him, and still express his maximum of possible power.

"How many great minds, irremediably destroyed by misguided voluptuousness," says M. Jean Finot, "are cut down before having expended for the human race one-tenth of their knowledge."

The same author, in his "Problems of the Sexes," quoting Sainte-Beuve, in deploring this waste of creative power caused by sexual dissipation, says: "Who shall say how, in a great city, at certain hours of the evening and the night, there are periodically exhausted treasures of genius, of beautiful and beneficent works, or fruitful fancies? One in whom, under rigid continence, a sublime creation of mind was about to unfold, will miss the hour, the passage of the star, the kindling moment which will nevermore be found. Another, inclined by nature to kindness, to charity, and to a charming tenderness, will become cowardly, inert, or even unfeeling. This character, which was almost fixed, will be dissipated and volatile."

Upon the proper use and conservation of " sexual force the progress of civilization itself depends. All history shows that just in proportion as the sex instinct is kept sacred, pure, and the life essence properly used and converted into creative, productive power, does a nation reach a high state of civilization. Wherever this instinct becomes generally perverted, as it did in ancient Rome, people become devitalized, lose their physical and mental stamina, and rapidly deteriorate. Where it is protected by virtue and purity of life, the nation rises in the scale of civilization; where it is abused, perverted, the nation sinks to the level of low-flying ideals.

In the last analysis of success, the mainspring of achievement must rest in the strength of a man's vitality; for without a stock of health equal to great emergencies and consistent longevity even the greatest ambition is comparatively powerless. Dissipation and impure living steal the energies, weaken the nature, lower the standards, blur the ideals, undermine the ambition, and lessen the whole vitality and power of a man.

This is true not only of physical, but also of mental impurity, for nothing is truer than that "To be carnally minded (sensually minded) is death." There are multitudes of people who break the seventh commandment mentally, who are injured as much as if they had broken it physically. Mental debauch is in some respects more disastrous in its effects than physical debauch. Lascivious longings, emotions that run riot, uncontrolled, are most demoralizing to the character. Some of the worst nerve diseases are really nothing but sexual neurosis, brought on by lascivious imaginings, unlawful mental revelings. Those whom we may well call sexual neurotics are unbalanced, selfish, usually cold-blooded, and lack all sense of proportion. They are driven under impulse, committing all sorts of criminal deeds.

The mind should be kept as unstained as the body. Every part of the being should be regarded as too holy to tamper with, too sacred to abuse, for the integrity or purity of each part of one's organism has a direct bearing upon the integrity, purity, and efficiency of every other part.

If a person who has always previously been honest commits one contemptible, dishonorable act, the texture of his entire character seems 1 to be changed thereafter. In a far more serious degree is this true in regard to the sex instinct. It is not like a mistake or a blunder, however serious, that may be made in any other direction. This would not materially change the life structure; but, when one deliberately violates his sex instinct, the tainted leaven never ceases to work until it permeates the whole man. No human being has ever been great enough to practice immorality, to tamper with his sexual nature, without suffering very serious mental and moral deterioration.

Impurity, because of its blighting, deadening influence upon the mental as well as the moral faculties, very seriously interferes with one's success in life. Not only does it undermine self-confidence, but it also takes the bloom from life, robs it of that buoyancy, spontaneity and effervescence which are the products of virtuous living, pure thoughts, a clean mind in a clean body.

Sexual indulgence not only saps the physical, the mental and the moral vitality; but it also takes the spring out of life, the force, the resilience. It destroys freshness, enthusiasm, the impulse to do and to be one's best.

A Roman emperor used to have the right hand cut off of every prisoner who was captured in war so that the men could not fight again; but this same mutilation also destroyed their productive power so that they were not as useful citizens as before. Sexual vice is more cruel than this pagan emperor. It not only cuts off the right hand of its victim's efficiency, but it also murders the man in him, leaving nothing but the shell of his former beauty and grand possibilities.

The human beings who have attained to the highest and most glorified perfection have been those in whom sex integrity had been preserved in all its purity. It is man's relation to divinity which paints the best part of the picture, which writes the divinest thing in authorship and in poetry. It is the sublimest part of genius, of creative energy. It is that which sparkles in the eye and is that which furnishes the sweetness and light in the lover's glances. It is a source of the sweetest thing in friendship. It is that which gives virility, vigor, strength and sweetness to human acts and human endeavor.

Men are most efficient, most vigorous, when they think most of themselves, when they have the greatest respect for themselves, and we are all so constituted that we cannot respect ourselves unless we do right.

A man is a giant when he can look himself and the world in the face without wincing; but he is a weakling when he is conscious that his self-respect is gone, that the ermine of his character is soiled, polluted. He has a fearful sense of mutilation and shame, of lost power. Many a man has been kept from doing a giant's work because of the consciousness of wrong-doing, which has shorn him of his power; so that, considering it from the most selfish standpoint alone, impurity generates inferiority, weakness, paralysis of energy, the killing of ambition, the bestializing of the ideal, the lowering of the moral and physical standards, —in short, the loss of manhood, the loss of womanhood.

Purity is the corner-stone, the very foundation of character; for, without purity, there can be no sterling quality, and without quality there can be no superiority.

Even the lower animals have no respect for the impure man, the loose liver. F. C. Bostock, the celebrated trainer of wild animals, says, "In some curious, incomprehensible way, wild animals know instinctively whether men are addicted to bad habits. It is one of the many problems that are beyond human understanding. For those who are in the least inclined to drink, or who live a loose life, a wild animal has neither fear nor respect. He despises them with all the contempt of his nature and recognizes neither their authority nor their superiority. If a man has begun to take just a little intoxicating liquor or has deviated from the straight road, animals will discover it long before his fellowmen. The quality in the trainer which dominates the animal nature within himself is precisely the quality which dominates the animal he trains. If he yields to the brute within him, no matter how little, his perfect poise and self-mastery are gone and the keen instinct of the wild beast recognizes this instantly. Brutes seem to understand man's degradation to their level, and his life is in danger every moment he is in their cage."

An impure man is never out of danger. He is perpetually risking his life in a den of wild beasts which he harbors within. Nothing is as pernicious; nothing will so quickly undermine the mental, the physical, and the moral life as impure practices, vicious habits. We all know how rapidly those who live impure live bum out and deteriorate physically and age prematurely. Impurity is decay. Impurity is death.

Multitudes manage to get along in comparative comfort and many have even achieved great success in spite of painful bodily afflictions ; but, as physicians well know, when there is anything wrong with the sexual life, it affects the mind even more than the body. Many impure men have gone to insane asylums, have committed suicide, or have been so afflicted with worry, mental depression, and despondency that they have not been able to do any effective work.

I have known a girl (and there are multitudes of similar cases), who stood very high in her community, a conscientious church worker, who became so completely transformed in a single year, after she had been betrayed and abandoned by a man she loved and trusted, that it did not seem possible she could be the same human being. No other sin could have wrought such terrific changes in her nature in so brief a time.

There is something about the sexual instinct which strikes at the very root of our nature, the very marrow of our being. It is the very essence of character; and, when this instinct is preserved in all its integrity, the integrity of absolute purity, when the sexual life is kept wholesome, healthy and robust, the whole life blossoms out in beauty and glory, but when it is perverted, abused, or misused, when its sacredness is gone, everything else seems to go with it.

A prominent writer says, "If young persons poison their bodies and corrupt their minds with vicious courses, no lapse of time, after a reform, is likely to restore them to physical soundness and the soul purity of their earlier days."

The sexual taint seems to be indelible. Not even religion is able to wipe it entirely out, for the bitter memory of past excesses haunts the individual clear to his grave; the horrible picture mocks one even at the point of death. We cannot tell why this is, but it would appear that Nature herself takes revenge for the violation of the sex instinct, implanted in man for the continuance of the race.

Many people seem to think that if their acts are pure and clean, so far as the public is concerned, it does not matter what they do privately. The privacy of the deed has nothing to do with the results to ourselves. A shepherd once saw an eagle soar out from a crag. It flew majestically up far into the sky, but by and by became unsteady and began to waver and wobble in its flight. First one wing dropped, then the other, and at length the poor bird fell to the ground. The shepherd sought the fallen bird and found that a little serpent had fastened itself upon it while resting on the crag. Unseen, unfelt, by the eagle, the serpent crawled in through its feathers, and while the proud monarch was sweeping through the air the reptile's fangs were thrust into its flesh, poisoning its blood, and bringing it reeling to the earth. It is the story of many a life. Some secret sin has long been eating its way into the heart, and at last the proud life lies soiled and dishonored in the dust.

Without purity there can be no lasting greatness. Vice honeycombs the physical strength and destroys also the moral fiber. Now and again the community is shocked and . startled when some man of note topples with a crash to sudden ruin and death. Yet the cause of the moral collapse is not sudden in its operation. There has been a slow undermining of virtue, a gradual poisoning of the very life centers going on for years. Then, perhaps, in an hour when honor, truth or honesty is brought to a crucial test, the weakened character gives way and there is an appalling commercial or social crash which too often finds an echo in the revolver shot of the suicide.

There never was a more beautiful prayer than that of the poor, soiled, broken-hearted psalmist in his hour of shame and repentance,— "Create in me a clean heart." "Who shall ascend into the hill of the Lord, who shall stand in His holy place? He that hath clean hands and a pure heart." There are thousands of men in this country to-day who would cut off their right hands to be free from the stain, the poison of impurity with which they became tainted in youth.

It is not a figure of speech to say "Purity is power." It is literally true. Purity is the very essence of our being, of forcefulness, of masterfulness.

There is nothing else which will whittle away the life quite so rapidly as indulgence in sexual vice. When a man is guilty of this sin all other bad things seem to rush to its aid to help pull him down. We sometimes see a tragic illustration of its destroying power in the case of the youth who is sent away from home to college. Overwhelmed by his new-found freedom he becomes sexually contaminated, plunges into other excesses, and in an incredibly short time goes down to ruin and death.

The impure age very rapidly. It is impossible to dissipate, especially in sexual vice, and keep young. It is well known that the women of the street are very short-lived,—that they only average four or five years in their miserable business. The violation of the most sacred thing in them so demoralizes and devitalizes their whole being, physically, mentally, morally, that the very consciousness of having killed the most precious thing they ever possessed rapidly grinds away their lives. Some of them age more in a single year than a girl who lives a pure life does in ten.

Purity is not only a health-preserver, but it is also a youth-preserver, a life-prolonger. The pure in heart realize the Scriptural promise,'—"His flesh shall be fresher than a child's. He shall return to the days of his youth."

Oh, no! we live our lives again;

For, warmly touched or coldly dim. The pictures of the past remain:

Man's works shall follow him.

—J. G. Whittier.

2
THE CRIME OF SILENCE

Self-reverence, self-knowledge, self-control. These three alone lead life to sovereign power. — Alfred Tennyson.

Virtue is an angel, but she is a blind one and must ask of knowledge to show her the pathway that leads to her goal. — Horace Mann.

"How it happened I can hardly understand," said a well-known man to me in confidence, "for when a boy I was very inquisitive and eager for information on every possible subject of inquiry; but, until I was more than twelve years old, I do not think that I had given even a passing thought to sexual matters. I had heard a few "smutty" stories, it is true, but they had no suggestive significance of lasciviousness to me, and were interesting or not only in proportion as they were merely intellectually witty. Perhaps my escape was largely due to the fact that, when active, I was so full of life and so engrossed in sport that there was no chance to talk to me about anything besides the game at issue, when I was playing, for I played with all my might and gave my playmates all they could attend to to prevent my beating them. When I was not active physically, I at once plunged into some book, for I was a great reader and could so concentrate my mind that I could read undisturbed with seven brothers and sisters playing around me, so long as they did not touch me.

"But one day a sudden, violent thunder shower drove me to shelter with two companions under an old shed, where we had to remain about two hours. The conversation drifted from one thing to another until one of the boys asked me if I had ever practiced self-abuse, calling it by a name common among the young. I did not even understand what he meant, and told him so; whereupon he explained his meaning, and added that I ought to try it, for I did not know what a good thing I was missing.

"Yet, even after this, it was several weeks before I did try it, and curiosity rather than inclination was the impelling motive. Of course I repeated the act, but soon realized that in some way I did not comprehend it was injuring me and reducing my abounding vivacity, so I decided to stop it. But somehow I did not stop, and then came the most sickening and terrifying consciousness I have ever experienced, as it suddenly dawned upon me that I was in the remorseless grip of a cruel habit. But I continued, though I felt much as the dying western stage driver must have felt when he cried out, in the delirium of fever, "I'm on the down grade, and I can't reach the brake!' "I had had the best of religious as well as intellectual training, and I remember thinking, one day, to myself, "Your soul is no longer your own! It is no use for you to talk of such things as God and heaven, for they are not for you! You are worse off than a slave,—worse off than if you were chained, as St. Paul said, to the body of death,—for you are by your own . deeds dragging out the most miserable of lives and seem bound to go down to the most miserable of graves. Is this all you are good for? Is this what you were created for? No, I was born for better things, and I will not become the ghastly victim of this cruel devil that seems to possess me now! It was a hard struggle— to get and keep my hand on 'the brake,'—but I finally won, although I cannot think even now without a mental shudder of the starless midnight of despair which seemed to be closing down upon me."

If this was the experience of one who drifted into this practice solely through curiosity, without any original temptation of inclination, what must have been that of thousands, perhaps millions, of others of naturally prurient susceptivities? If, struggling against it with all his might, he barely escaped, how about others of weaker wills who have not become alarmed so soon? Where were all the "guardians and protectors" of the young that they gave him no warning or instruction in such matters?—where were parents, schools, churches, the state, philanthropists, and others commonly supposed to be deeply interested in the welfare of youth? Think of building a powerful locomotive or steamship and putting it upon the track or the ocean, as the case may be, with all steam turned on, but without giving the captain any chart or map to sail by, or the engineer any idea of the time schedule or the meaning of the danger signals along the line!

"The idea that ignorance is essential to innocence is happily being exploded," says Dr. Irving D. Steinhardt, "and we physicians are in a better position than the laity to speak of the wreckage and disaster that result from ignorance and neglect of proper instruction on sex hygiene."

I know of nothing which has wrecked the happiness and lives of more young people than our foolish prudery, our criminal silence, regarding the most vital facts of their being, facts which underlie the very foundation of society. How little you fathers and mothers who remain silent on the all-important subject of sex life realize the painful and humiliating experiences, the terrible suffering and wreckage, which your silence may be laying up for your children in the years to come. If you could follow them into the future—follow them to the confessional, to their clergymen, to their physicians, to the operating table; if you could only hear them years hence pouring into the ears of their priests, their pastors, their doctors, the woes of their blighted lives, you would certainly learn a lesson which you would never forget. You would realize that, while it may be difficult for you now to speak on this delicate subject to your children, your silence is putting a terrible premium on their ignorance, a premium which may cost them untold future suffering, which may bring tragedy into their homes when they marry, and may entail disease worse than death upon their children.

We are only just beginning to recognize and appreciate the tremendous modifying power of the sex element in the growing boy and girl, the body-changing, mind-changing, character-molding influence of the sexual organs.

Accidents or surgical operations resulting in the destruction of the sexual glands in the boy, say of ten or twelve years of age or a little older, cause radical changes in everything which marks sex distinction. The voice becomes thin and squeaky and the muscles grow flabby and soft; the chest instead of developing becomes narrow, the shoulders often slope and the mind loses its virility. In other words, the boy becomes mentally as well as physically emasculated. He has lost his stamina and the very characteristics which mark the strong man and he becomes feminine. In fact, if he were dressed like a girl he would pass for one, but a very weak, characterless one.

Equally radical changes take place in the girl who loses her ovaries. Her fine, delicate feminine characteristics begin to disappear, and she takes on the very masculine qualities which the emasculated youth loses. Her physique, her muscles, her voice become masculine, heavy, coarse. She often takes on an enormous amount of fat, and in fact completely loses her comely feminine form. And she, just as the boy in girls' clothes would pass for a girl, in male attire would pass for a man, but a very inferior man.

In short, the emasculated boy loses his virility and masculinity and the emasculated girl her femininity and attractiveness; each loses the peculiar charm and distinction of sex.

The unfortunate thing is that the emasculated male is neither a man nor a woman, nor the emasculated female either a woman or a man. Each develops weakened characteristics of the opposite sex.

Can any other knowledge then be half so important as this knowledge of oneself, of one's nature, which makes one what he or she is, a knowledge which may make all the difference between a mongrel, a half animal and half human being, and a magnificent man or a superb woman!

The time will come when to keep such knowledge away from a boy or girl will be considered not only cruel but criminal. The only possible way of improving the race and of preventing untold misery and horrible tragedies caused by sex wastage, sexual abuse, is through proper instruction of the youth.

There is no other subject a hundredth part so important to youths as that of the sex instinct and the relations of the sexes, about which parents have hitherto preserved such foolish silence. They have been careful to teach their children in religious matters; they have been particular about their going to church and to Sunday School, about their mental development, what they study and what they read; they have been anxious for them to associate with cultured people in order that they might acquire good breeding, but concerning the great facts of their sexual life, facts which speak so loudly in their nature, which clamor so persistently and insistently for recognition, they have had nothing to say. Practically all their children have learned regarding this subject is by inference, from vulgar jokes and innuendoes, all sorts of distorted information which they pick up from questionable sources (which only arouses a morbid and most vicious curiosity), but not a particle of instruction have they received from the people they respect and revere and to whom they have a right to look for safeguarding instruction.

I know many parents who, through some fatally mistaken idea of modesty, lack the moral courage frankly to tell their children the truth about their sex nature, and who try to get teachers or friends to broach the subject to them. Do you realize, my parent friends, that when you delegate this sacred duty to others you are weakening that most precious of all bonds between child and parent,—that unquestioned confidence and sweet trust which Nature has implanted in the heart of the child, who in his tenderest years looks up to his parents as authorities on all matters? Isn't it infinitely better to put aside your false modesty and teach your children the true and beautiful meaning of sex than to hazard their future happiness and efficiency, or to hear in after years that bitter cry which has gone up from many a young soul in extremity of anguish: "Oh, why did not my parents tell me the truth about myself! Why did they not hang out the danger signal upon the sex rocks and reefs before it was too late"

Isn't it a thousand times better that your children should learn the truth about themselves from those who love them as their own lives, than to get a confused idea of it from the vicious insinuations and vile suggestions of those who associate with them in the street or at school?

Some parents flatter themselves that their children are safe in private schools, where only the best boys and girls are supposed to be; but in most private schools, as in most other schools and colleges, sexual demoralization is more or less rife. How often it has happened that a single sexual pervert has contaminated the morals of an entire school, and the pity of it is that the harm is usually done before even the teachers know of it. The mischief is carried on so secretly, the evil is so subtle, the impurity leaven is so insidious that the whole character is often honeycombed before the teachers or the parents find it out.

Mothers who think it is a terrible thing to post children in sex matters, who think that they should find out these things themselves, little realize how often it happens that their own little daughters, even in the primary-school, or later in private schools or seminaries, are already sexually contaminated because of their ignorance.

"Nearly fifteen years in the Juvenile Court convinces me," says Judge Benjamin Lindsey, "that there is hardly one child out of one hundred who has reached the age of twelve that hasn't come in contact with some sort of sex experience, either through vulgar stories or that sort of curiosity that is more or less natural and to be expected with a growing child. I used to think that this was true with more particular reference to boys; but I am convinced— as is also the lady assistant judge of this court (who has sat with me in girls' cases for more than ten years)—that it is almost equally true of girls. We are almost constantly having to shock mothers with disclosures concerning the sex immorality of their daughters because of the cases that have to come under the observation of the officers of the Juvenile Court."

This statement of Judge Lindsey's should arouse every father and mother to the necessity of sex instruction. If you Have not properly instructed them, it is always safe to presume that your boys and girls, unless very small, have picked up a great deal more of information regarding sex matters than you have any idea of. Your silence on these matters does not keep them innocent of the vulgar, distorted side of the sex subject. They get this in spite of you, and the pity of it all is that they do not have your instruction to neutralize and take the attractiveness out of this luridly colored information. Unfortunately, there are always human brutes who are ready to put into the minds of the young all sorts of vile insinuations, half-truths, and vicious suggestions, sensual insinuations, and to put into their hands foul literature and lewd pictures. There are always those who take pleasure in feeding the curiosity of the young upon distorted sex knowledge which simply inflames the passions and develops a morbid imagination.

Sexual dangers lie largely in the very secrecy maintained by those who should give instruction on the whole subject. But Nature herself will not tolerate ignorance on this matter; she forces knowledge regarding it. The imperious questioning, the insistent desires, the call of awakening passion, of burgeoning youth demand an explanation. Who is going to give this explanation? That rests with you parents. If you do not give it to them, your children will pick up whatever sex information they can, wherever they can, out of your sight and hearing. Information thus acquired is never clean, pure and wholesome, as it would be if it came from the right source, but always gross and vulgar, always discolored with low, sensual, lecherous suggestion.

One of the great objections to posting youth regarding their sex nature is that it will tend to arouse a morbid curiosity. Now I believe, on the contrary, that a knowledge of the scientific facts, simply, freely and frankly imparted, at the right age and with tact, is the only thing that will prevent the possibility of morbid curiosity on the subject. Children are only curious about that which is concealed. A frank, open discussion will dispel any morbid curiosity. It is the hidden truth, that which is clothed in mystery, that arouses curiosity.

Has it ever occurred to you that your children must think it strange that this wonderful subject of sex, which interests them more than anything else during their perilous years, is one that is never mentioned at home, never so much as referred to and that the very reasons which brought their father and mother together, made them live together as husband and wife, are never even referred to? Even in homes where parents constantly joke the children about their sweethearts and about getting married, the principles that underlie this wonderful, mysterious subject are never explained, but unfortunately the sex-consciousness is morbidly developed, and the young people are left in darkness and ignorance to wrestle with their instincts and passions as best they can. The boy and the girl feel that they must keep their thoughts concealed from everybody for whom they have any respect, because they never hear those whom they love and admire referring to the subject. It is only the vicious and the low who will talk about it to them.

Now, when your children ask questions upon sex matters, before they have developed a morbid self-consciousness in regard to the subject, why make a mystery of it ? Why evade them or fill their minds with fables and lies? Why not answer them frankly and truthfully ? They will find out the truth sooner or later, and will then think less of you for having deceived them. Furthermore, when they get this information from outside, as they are bound to if parents refuse to give it to them, father or mother will never again be the same confidant as before. Your children will gradually drift away, and, more or less, estrangement will grow up between you.

Remember that the relation of your child to you through its dependent years, when it looks up to you in implicit faith, is such that he will never again, probably, have the same confidence in information given by anyone else. Then is your priceless opportunity to tell him the straight truth. To refuse to guide him in these impressionable, perilous years is as cruel as it would be to let a blind man wander in a street which would lead him into a river.

If you can manage to be such a close confidant of your boy that he will instinctively and naturally come to you with every question which troubles him, and always feel free to talk over the most intimate relations of his life with you, you will have little to fear for his future. If you instill into your child's mind, in such a way that it will never be eradicated, the idea that he should never do anything which he would be ashamed to have his mother know all about, you have accomplished a wonderful thing.

Most parents have an idea that imparting sexual knowledge to children is like brushing the bloom from the peach, that it means the loss of early innocence. There could not be a greater mistake. The whole subject can be so handled that it will seem just as natural to get instruction on it as on any other. It can be treated in so pure and simple a manner that a child would regard a filthy reference or low joke in connection with it as he would an insulting jest regarding his mother.

The main thing in imparting sex instruction to a boy and girl is to do it in a delicate as well as simple way, to avoid coarseness and crudity and every possibility of the youthful imagination visualizing pictures of sexual sin.

Many well-meaning writers who are trying to help young people to solve their sex problems approach the subject in such a roundabout, mysterious manner that they give the impression that there really is something to be ashamed of, something which must be concealed. While their motives are admirable, they do more harm than good. They make the mistake that the majority of grown people make, in thinking that children have deep or involved thoughts upon the subject. As a matter of fact, nothing is farther from the truth. Their ideas regarding it are very vague and their minds are very easily satisfied; but they should be satisfied along the line of truth and not of deception.

Nothing is gained and much is lost in deceiving a child or misleading him with fables of the stork flying in the window with the baby or the angels bringing it down from heaven. Children, as a rule, think of the matter in such vague and indefinite terms as are suggested in the question which one little fellow asked his mother, "Where was I when there wasn't any me?" Now, as it doesn't take very much to satisfy such a child's curiosity, why deceive him?—why mystify him?—why not, in simple, chaste language, tell him the truth? It can be done in such a delicate way as to satisfy his mind, without in the least distressing him or robbing him of a particle of his fresh innocence. Then, when he gets a little older, when his mind can grasp more truth, give him more, but do not wait until too late to give this instruction. Give it to him a little in advance of his sexual development. Then there will be no danger of developing a morbid imagination, unchaste visualizing. The plain facts, the truth, will free the young mind from all morbid curiosity. But, if you begin by deceiving him, you have got to continue; and, when he hears the truth in the wrong way from someone else, he loses confidence in you.

I believe that the mother is the safest link in connecting young children with this whole mystery of sex. Because of her mother love, superior tact, and marvelous instinct, there is little danger of her startling or shocking the awakening young mind. Men, generally, are more awkward in their language. They lack that delicacy of approach, that sensitiveness of mental touch, that fine intuition which is a part of the feminine nature. To children, especially when they are still young, there is nothing in this world so sacred as their mother. What she says carries infinitely more weight than what the father or the teacher says. When the boy approaches manhood, then the father may safely assume the office of confidant and instructor of his son in these matters, but during his very tender years the mother should be his guide.

The mother, in taking advantage of a favorable opportunity when her boy is in the right affectionate mood, can tell him the scientific facts of sex in such language that no unnatural suspicion or sensual suggestion will be aroused in his mind. Instead he will take the whole thing as a matter of course. Perhaps one or two little talks may not only save your boy from untold misery or the possible wreckage of his whole life, but may bind him to you closer than anything else that has ever come up between you. He will ever after say to himself, in moments of temptation, "My mother told me this," and it will mean infinitely more to him than knowledge obtained from any other source. It will bear the stamp of sacredness, of cleanness, of purity, and save him many a pitfall.

Or the whole question may be simply and naturally introduced by telling your child of the dignity and sacredness of motherhood. If a boy is properly instructed in regard to this, and a high ideal of womanhood is roused in him, he can safely be given the scientific facts regarding his physical being, and the natural, normal generation and reproduction of human life.

The mother can explain the facts of maternity, the mystery of it all, as no one else can. Let her impress the boy with the sanctity of motherhood, and the awful sacrifice which every mother makes in bringing a child into the world. Let her teach him that her very suffering so intensifies the mother's love for her child that she would gladly give her life to protect it. This will strengthen his love for his mother and build up his ideal of the holiness, the beauty and the wonder of it all.

Beautiful sex lessons can be taught children through botany and zoology. It is not a very difficult matter to teach boys and girls about the marvelous provision made by Nature for the reproduction and perpetuation of life in plants, in fishes, in the lower animals, and in human beings. Begin with the egg, the origin of the chicken, or the fish, the metamorphosis of the insect, and the fertilization of plants. All this will lead up easily and naturally to human reproduction and the natural instinct of all animals for pairing, with the object of the perpetuation of the species, and how this pairing in the lower forms of life foreshadows the home.

The introduction of this subject will give the intelligent mother an opportunity to instill into the mind of her children lessons from the evolution of life and the progress of the world. She can go back to the time when there were no human beings on the earth, and show her little ones how our highest specimens of manhood have gradually been evolved from animal forms so low as to be scarcely distinguishable from vegetable organisms. She can explain how man has been foreshadowed in other forms of life and how Nature for millions of years has been evolving higher and higher organisms up to the highest human type of the present.

She can picture to them how man has climbed from the Hottentots to the Gladstones, the Washingtons, the Lincolns, and fill their young imagination with all the wonders of evolution.

Where the mother has not been scientifically instructed in these things herself, she can give her children all the facts she knows in regard to the subject in a sweet, natural way which will forewarn and safeguard them from a thousand perilous experiences. When they are older, especially if the home is in a city or town, where they have the advantage of a public library, text books, giving elementary instruction on physiology, anatomy and kindred subjects may be given them. Later, when their minds are thus prepared, they can be introduced to the plain truths of sex physiology, sex anatomy and sex hygiene, as presented by the best authorities.

While giving this sex instruction and information the whole object should be to enlarge the children's horizon, to uplift their ideas of Nature, of law and of religion, while at the same time instilling into their young minds the wonder, the miracle, the sacredness of the marvelous works of God, especially of the powers locked up within themselves.

Many of you fathers and mothers will say that the very suggestion that you talk over sex matters with your children is repulsive, that these are things that should not be thought of by the young, to say nothing of talking them over with them; that the discussion of this subject would only fill their minds with forbidden thoughts. But let me tell you that there is not a thousandth part the risk or danger in telling your boys and girls the entire facts of their own sexual life and the miracle of reproduction that there is in silence and secrecy. Indeed, a pure and scientific knowledge of those important facts is a protection against evil, against morbid curiosity and forbidden thoughts. It is ignorance not sex facts but imagined sex matters that are dangerous, perilous; knowledge means protection, safety.

Do not make the mistake that so many parents seem to commit in taking ignorance for purity. Purity is in constant danger unless it is protected by the sort of knowledge that will safeguard it. Our mothers are pure, our wives are pure, but it is not the purity of ignorance. Impurity is often the result of ignorance.

Few parents begin to realize what the curiosity of a child means, and what it will lead to in this matter if not satisfied in a wholesome and normal manner by proper instruction. The minds of children, as everyone knows, are filled with interrogation points on all subjects. How do you think they can be reared in a home without knowing something of the relation of the opposite sexes? The manner of living of their father and mother, the babies coming into the home, and other facts of life cannot be hidden from them. Children are not blind, and they are naturally more inquisitive about those things which are purposely kept from them.

Boys and girls know that when they arrive at a certain age they are kept apart for some reason, that there is a radical difference between the sexes. They cannot understand the reason for all this silence and mystery; for, while everything else is talked about, a veil is drawn over all sex matters. They wonder why you stammer and blush whenever the subject is broached, or try to put them off with all sorts of indirectness and fables, or pass it over in jest.

If the life you are leading is legitimate and right, if the generation and perpetuation of life are legitimate and sacred things, why do you seem ashamed of them? By your silence you appear to indicate that even the best people in the world are living in a manner which is not right, and that the Creator has decreed that some functions of the body, though necessary, are not as sacred as others.

The whole training of our children is calculated to give them a totally wrong impression of the sex relation. The criminal silence of parents, together with the unholy, vulgar insinuations and suggestions which they absorb on the street, in the schools, and in all sorts of places outside the home tend to impress upon children the idea that there is something not only marvelously mysterious about it, but also something unclean and wicked. Then they go to church and hear the exposition of the doctrine that "we are all conceived in sin;" and, putting this fact with the mysterious silence of fathers and mothers, they conclude that there is something even in the relation of their parents which must not be alluded to. Then, as the boy especially grows toward youth and manhood, he sees and hears about the awful degradation of the underworld, the sowing of wild oats, and other impure things, all of which information only mystifies him more and more, and further stimulates a morbid curiosity in regard to all other sex matters.

Indeed, one of the worst things about this criminal silence upon the sex question is that it often makes the sex impulse itself the youth's teacher, by arousing an insistent desire for light regarding this wonderful mystery; and he resorts to all sorts of questionable sources, impure associates, books and pictures which appeal to the vile and vicious in human nature to get the information he craves. He is thus led to listen to low, vulgar insinuations and innuendoes, which would simply disgust him if he had had clean, scientific knowledge on the subject. Not being safeguarded in a sane, wholesome way, his inflamed imagination runs away with him, and before he realizes it he is plunged into the very vice which would instinctively have repelled him had he been properly posted.

Had all children had clean, pure instruction upon this wonderful and sacred subject from the start, this morbid, vulgar side of it which permeates the very atmosphere of all vile places would never have developed.

Many a youth, when he begins to study medicine, has a lot of morbid sex curiosity; but, when he goes into the dissecting room and becomes familiar with the great truths of anatomy and physiology, when he realizes the marvelousness of the human machine, with all its complex functions, the facts of life become sacred to him. Morbid curiosity vanishes before the light of science. Distorted information has no more attractions for him, because he has seen into the very holy of holies of human life.

Is it not time that we treat it in a scientific way, that we turn on the light on this whole question? Is it not time that we put a stop to the discrediting of marriage, the most sacred of all human relations, and give our children pure information in place of the impure; scientific facts in the place of distorted knowledge, knowledge which tends to arouse morbid curiosity? The whole subject has been kept too long in the dark. Evil thrives in darkness, in ignorance. Light and knowledge are their antidotes. They will clean up the foulest of human cesspools.

It may be hard for you to overcome traditional custom and tell your boys and girls the truth about their own bodies, but ignorance of the subject may prove fatal. Their future depends upon their being properly instructed on these tabooed questions during the dangerous years when special temptations will come to them, and when they will need all the protection which the wisdom of your riper years and wider knowledge of human nature enables you to give them. Let them profit by your mistakes and any unfortunate experiences that may have come to you from ignorance in youth.

The question whether instruction in sex hygiene should be given in public schools is a burning one just now. We find teachers, college professors and clergymen ranged in opposite camps.

Professor Hugo Munsterberg, of Harvard University, says: "The cleanest boys and girls cannot give theoretical attention to their thoughts concerning sexuality without the whole mechanism for reinforcement automatically entering into action. We may instruct with the best intention to suppress, and yet our instruction itself must become a source of stimulation, which unnecessarily creates the desire for improper conduct."

Mrs. Ella Flagg Young, superintendent of the public schools of Chicago, on the other hand, says that their experiment in sex instruction in the schools of Chicago has increased the girls' sense of their own dignity and the marvelous meaning of their nature. The knowledge they are acquiring is taking the place of the silly ignorance which so long has been regarded as innocence, and the girls hold their heads higher and seem to think more of themselves. They have greater respect for their own bodies. , Only a short time ago the teaching of sex hygiene in Sunday Schools was approved in the report to the convention of the International Sunday School Association by E. K. Mohr, Superintendent of the Purity Department.

"Sex knowledge will be taught," said Mr. Mohr. "If not in the homes and the Sunday School, it will be taught in the street. Silence is criminal. We cannot remain inactive. We must teach these facts and teach them right, so that knowledge may lead to purity and righteousness.

"With the new awakening and discussion of sex matters, the pendulum has swung from silence to publicity that is almost nauseating. Literature, the stage, the newspapers, the 'movies' have exploited the interest in the subject. The endeavor to avoid false modesty may in the end break down the barriers of real modesty.

"With the religious atmosphere and reverent receptive attitude of the Sunday School, it is eminently fitted to bear the message of the knowledge that tends to personal purity. It is the plainest religious strategy."

I once knew a man of liberal education who, from being an honored member of a college faculty, had been dragged slowly down by the practice of self-abuse until he had no decided opinions on any subject of importance. He dropped, too, in the grade and character of the work he could and would do until he became and continued for a few years the caretaker of the lavatories in a large hotel.

Professor Henry, the bell boys called him, half in derision, half in respect for his evident inherent ability. Death finally closed his career in almost total mental vacuity. He had acquired the habit unwarned, as a boy; and, though it had been of slow growth for a few years, during which he climbed upward in life, it finally conquered and destroyed him.

It is a strange fact that many of the most highly educated and cultivated people are still reluctant to sanction even the discussion of sex life, except in medical circles. Teachers are seriously handicapped by parents' reticence; and, even while teachers feel that they could materially help the children, they hesitate to introduce the subject; whereas, if they knew that they were backed by the parents, they could do a great deal. I believe, however, that the time will come when sex instruction will be given in our schools, in connection with biology, hygiene, and ethics, and the evolution of the whole subject will be as natural and normal as that of any other study. I believe that no student should be allowed to graduate from college, or any other of our higher institutions of learning without passing a satisfactory examination upon the nature and meaning of the sexual instincts, so that the young man may be fitted to fulfill the holy office of husband and father, and the young woman the sacred office of wife and mother.

Some of the women's clubs in America are doing excellent work in providing courses for mothers and teachers; and, apart from the sensational exploitations of vice, there is an ever-increasing movement for the dissemination of wholesome knowledge on this most important of all matters touching the welfare of the race.

This movement is not confined to any particular locality or nationality. It is sweeping with irresistible force over the entire civilized world. It promises to tear off from society its mask of prudery and false modesty and to start youths and maidens out in life with pure, clean, scientific knowledge of their o bodies which will safeguard their health, their homes and future families. I believe that this universal campaign of sex hygiene is destined to bring more good to the human race than any other movement of modem times.

3
"DANGEROUS PASSING"

We paint, ourselves, the joy, the fear
Of which the coming life is made. And fill our future's atmosphere
With sunshine or with shade; The tissue of the life to be.
We weave with colors all our own; And, in the field of destiny,
We reap as we have sown.—J. G. Whittier.

So close does falsehood approach to truth that the wise man would do well not to trust himself on the narrow edge. —CICERO.

A POLICE inspector, in an address before New York public school graduates, said: "I have just come from the Tombs, where I closed the gates behind a wealthy murderer. I want to tell you, young men, that ninety-nine per cent, of the crimes committed to-day are caused by evil companions."

Familiarity with vulgarity tends to make us vulgar. Familiarity with evil, with immorality, robs it of its hideousness. What we have become accustomed to, we first give our consent to, then our approval. Those who associate with vile characters tend to become vile.

Investigation has shown that a very large percentage of those who have strayed from the path of virtue began their downfall through the fatal contagion of impurity communicated from vicious associates.

One who has made a special study of the effect of immorality upon men says that impure thought suggested by evil associates is one of the earliest indications of the downfall of character. He affirms that ninety-five per cent, of the men and boys in factories and places of manual labor boast of their impurity.

This seems an appalling statement, but it is supplemented by that of another investigator who says, "Seventy-five to eighty per cent, of men have, before marriage, been infected with some form of venereal disease." He adds that the truth of this "is widely accepted by medical authorities."

Under such conditions as these it is not difficult to imagine the danger of youth from impure associations-. Even clean, innocent, beautifully reared children, who seem so pure that nothing can contaminate them, are touched by the leper spot of vicious contagion when thrown into bad company, as the soundest and rosiest apples are soon infected when in contact with other apples which have begun to decay.

Impure suggestion is a youth's worst enemy. After an impure thought has once taken hold of the mind it requires strong will power to control one's desires. The trouble begins with the thought; hence the imperative importance of keeping with pure people, keeping in a pure, wholesome atmosphere, reading clean literature, because evil associations awaken forbidden inclinations. The suggestions of bad companions visualize the strongest temptations, and greatly increase the dangers that surround youth and innocence.

A boy who chooses for companions those who are already corrupted, who sneer at virtue, whose ideals are low flying, who actually boast of their impurity, cannot escape the pollution that invariably results from such associations. "Evil communications corrupt good manners," says a well-known proverb. Even more do they corrupt good morals. On the other hand, just as surely does the boy who selects his friends among those who are clean, wholesome, pure-minded, who aims to be somebody and to do something in the world, who has no secret companions to whom he would not introduce his sister or his mother,—just as surely does such a boy incline toward all that is noble, pure, and uplifting.

There is as strong an affinity between evil things as between good things. All forms of dissipation belong to the same family, and there is a strong probability, amounting almost to certainty, that the boy who is introduced to a single vicious practice by evil companions will be initiated into the whole family of evil things.

Judges in children's courts tell us that nearly every boy who goes wrong begins with smoking cigarettes. While we know that thousands of men who smoke are pure and clean in their lives, yet it is a fact that learning to smoke is usually a boy's initiation into wrongdoing. Smoking has a much more demoralizing influence upon a boy, because of his immaturity, than upon a man. This is especially true if he learns to smoke during the dangerous years of puberty, when he already has all the natural temptations which he Is able to withstand. Although it is not as vicious in its influence as intoxicating drinks, yet somehow nicotine, especially in youth, is very often the entering wedge which opens the door to alcohol, other deadly drugs, and sexual sins. All bad things seem to be linked together. All forms of dissipation, vice, and crime go hand in hand. Their affinity draws them together. This is what makes it so difficult to reform a person when he is started downhill, just as the affinity of all that is good and pure and clean tends to draw a man up when he is going in that direction, when he is trained with the family of good influences.

Somebody has said that the common expression "They all do it" is the devil's other name. Innumerable life tragedies have resulted from the suggestion of "they all do it." Young people have a morbid dread of refusing to do the things their companions do, even when they know they are wrong. Trying to be a good fellow, to do as "the other fellows" did has proved the gateway to ruin for many a boy. How many youths are ashamed to refuse to smoke a cigarette, or a cigar, or to "take a drink," because their companions think it is manly to smoke and drink.

It is true that it often takes a great deal of courage for a youth to refuse to yield to temptation, to rebuke impurity or vulgarity, or to show his disgust and disapprobation of an impure suggestion or a questionable story. He fears the ridicule of his companions. But the moral bravery that frowns on such things is the strongest proof of real manliness, and wins the admiration even of those who laugh and jeer at it.

I remember a young man who had been appointed to an important position and who was given a "send-off" by his young friends. At the dinner in his honor questionable stories and suggestions were repeated. Toasts had been drunk to girls with whom 4ome of the young men had improper relations, when the guest of the evening was asked to speak. He raised his glass and said: "I drink a toast to my mother!" This pointed rebuke put an end to all the questionable proceedings.

As some perverted taste develop a preference for tainted meats, so many men seem to prefer a tainted story, a tainted book, a tainted picture, a vulgar joke, or a low, foul insinuation. Their diseased imaginations revel in filth, until they lose their taste entirely for the sweet, the pure, the beautiful, the normal.

When boys lose their love and appreciation for clean humor and laugh at impure stories and coarse vulgar suggestions and jokes, it is a pretty sure indication that they are in danger, that they have been sexually contaminated, and have formed vicious associations or habits. People who tell immoral stories and revel in vulgar innuendoes are on the downward track.

"A great trait of Grant's character," said George W. Childs, 'Vas his purity. I never heard him express an impure thought, or make an indelicate allusion. There is nothing I ever heard him say that could not be repeated in the presence of women. When President, if a man was brought up for an appointment, and it was shown that he was an immoral man. Grant would not appoint him, no matter how great the pressure brought to bear." Many instances characteristic of the great general's answer to impure stories are on record. On one occasion, when he formed one of a dinner party of American gentlemen in a foreign city, conversation drifted to questionable matters, when he suddenly rose and said, "Gentlemen, please excuse me; I will retire."

"I have such a rich story that I want to tell you," said an officer who, one evening during the Civil War, came into the Union camp in a rollicking mood. "There are no ladies present, are there?" General Grant, lifting his eyes from the paper which he was reading, and looking the officer squarely in the eye, said, slowly and deliberately: "No, hut there are gentlemen present/'

A manly man is Nature's gentleman, the only true gentleman, and he will no more pollute his lips by repeating an impure story or joke than will Nature's gentlewoman, a womanly woman. Neither will associate with, or make companions of those who take pleasure in such things, who delight in what is gross, low, immoral.

You cannot touch pitch without being defiled. You cannot associate with the impure without catching the taint of their impurity, their sensualism, their lust, poisons which act like a leaven in the whole nature. The mind, responding to the law of suggestion, soon adopts what it is familiar with; and, before you realize it, you fall into the vicious practices of your companions. This is one of the dangers of college life, of being led into false paths by youths who are morally tainted, but who have brilliant or magnetic qualities that draw others to them, or by the large class of wealthy students, rotten at the core, who have made some of our institutions of learning hotbeds of dissipation.

In order to be safe from moral contagion, one must as far as possible keep away from temptation, away from people, from books, from pictures, from places, from anything which can possibly suggest a particle of impurity. Then the battle for self-control, for the mastery of unruly passions, will be an easy one. There is nothing to be gained by putting yourself in a position where you will be constantly straining your self-control, straining your will power, which may be weak, where you will be continually fighting against vicious suggestions. A youth who keeps his mind absolutely pure has the whip hand over his passions. It is the impure thought that irritates, that generates the secretions which produce the passion.

As long as the thought is pure the body will take care of itself.

Every impure thought or experience affects the whole body through the mind. A sensual thought makes a sensual, beastly body. A person who practices impurity doesn't realize that he is brutalizing his body, sensualizing his mind, vulgarizing his own nature; that, after a time, everybody who comes in contact with him feels his animalism. No one can successfully cover up the taint of continued impurity. Nor can he resist its mental ravages. While the mental faculties become weaker and weaker, the passions become stronger and more inflamed and goad the weak will on to excesses which result in terrible demoralization, degeneration of both the physical and the moral being.

We are so constructed that everything that is worthwhile, everything that we prize most, everything that elevates, costs us something. We must pay for it in effort, and it is precious in proportion to the struggles and the sacrifices which we make to obtain it. A youth who would keep himself "unspotted from the world," especially a city youth, must be constantly on his guard against the snares and temptations which surround him.

"Look out! Paint!" wrote the keeper of a beer garden on a large card which he tacked up at the entrance to his premises. But he was a poor penman, his rude "P" looked for all the world like a "T," and those who saw it read, "Look out! Taint!" Yet it was a most appropriate notice, for the danger from taint within was far greater than from paint without. Look out, young man; beware, young woman, before you enter such places. Only too often, whole lives are tainted therein as badly as one rotting vegetable taints others around it.

In the alleys, the byways, the closed streets of our cities we often see the sign, "Dangerous Passing." Although not in written characters, we can see this sign all along the pathway of life. We read it over the street and avenue that leads to vice and degradation; we read it over doors that lead to saloons and gambling hells, and dens of infamy. We read it in front of all the pleasures which are forbidden or doubtful.

"Dangerous Passing." We read it in the deformed and crippled lives of those who have disregarded its warning, in the botched, demoralized and bungling work of the weak and inefficient. We read it in the ruined lives and lost opportunities and blighted hopes of those who would not heed it. We see it in all those who lead irregular or dissipated lives, who exhaust their vitality in youth. We read it in nervous wrecks, in brain trouble, insanity. We read it in the hesitating step, in the wrinkles of the prematurely old, in those who carry about in their bodies unmistakable signs which are the results of not heeding the warning, "Dangerous Passing."

Be careful how you disregard the danger sign which Nature puts up, her warning of the "dangerous passing" place where justice, forgiveness, mercy and even love are left behind.

4

"A LITTLE DEVIL TO PLAY WITH"

'Tis life, not death for which we pant: 'Tis life, whereof our nerves are scant; More life and fuller that we want.

— Alfred Tennyson.

"Mother if I'm not naughty; if I am really a very good boy, will God let me have just one little devil to play with when I go to Heaven?"

This question was put to his mother by a little fellow of five. To a student of child life it is more pathetic than funny, signifying, as it does, that the idea of real happiness, joy, and freedom from restraint was associated in the mind of this child with evil.

It is possible to so train children that vice will seem attractive and virtue undesirable. In multitudes of homes they are brought up on goody-goody philosophy, to the entire exclusion of all the natural instincts of childhood. Not only does this sort of training not appeal to the children, but it prejudices them against the very things which the philosophy is supposed to inculcate.

Nor is this inclination toward evil, as sparks fly upward, confined only to the young. There is a strange element of perversity in all human nature which often impels us to do the very things we know in our heart of hearts may be bad for us,—may be even fatal for us. This it is which impels and seems almost irresistibly to force some people standing on the brink of a precipice to throw themselves over. Said a highly educated, moral, mature lady once at the French court, as she held to the light a glass of pure, sparkling water, "Oh, if it were only wicked to drink this, how nice it would be!"

It is idle to say, however true, that people should themselves conquer all such inclinations and ideas. It is also incumbent upon us, who are supposedly superior to all such weaknesses, to help keep them away from the brink of such a precipice.

You cannot bring children up on the husks of righteousness, and the very essence of the religion of childhood, of all religion, is joy, gladness, cheerfulness, bubbling, optimistic life. Theology doesn't appeal to children, but life does; Nature does; all the beautiful things the Creator has given us for use and enjoyment fill the heart of a child with gladness.

"I am so full of happiness," said one in a spontaneous outburst of joy, "that I could not be any happier unless I could grow."

As a rule the happiest children make not only the happiest, but also the most useful men and women. We cannot give children too much real fun, too much heart sunshine, too much love. They thrive on such things. They are their normal food, and the home is the place above all others where they should get an abundance of them.

Yet in many families the children are hungry for affection, as well as for amusement; but they get no encouragement; their play-loving instincts are constantly suppressed. They get no pleasure at home, no love from their parents, and they naturally seek these things elsewhere. I have known boys to go to the bad because their policeman parents put them under too strict surveillance. While unwilling to let them play and have a good time at home, they were so afraid they would get with bad boys and hear something that would contaminate them that they kept them shut up in the house, or in their own yards, until the youngsters rebelled and took advantage of every opportunity to get away and find "just one little devil to play with." And because they were denied the chance for self-expression that every normal child demands and requires, they found not one, indeed, but many little devils to play with!

There is a certain mysterious, subtle fascination in wrongdoing which cannot be explained, but it is something that especially appeals to children and young people who have been suppressed, over-guarded, over-watched by parents or guardians. Their curiosity is strengthened by repression, and they are constantly wanting to see what the forbidden things are like.

If children are allowed to give vent to all that is joyous and happy and spontaneous in their natures; if they are not continually repressed by "don'ts" in regard to legitimate things, the things they ought to have, they will be much less likely to be attracted to those that are forbidden, and they will be infinitely more likely to blossom out into helpful men and women, instead of becoming suppressed and sad-faced, if not depraved, individuals. Children who are encouraged in self-expression through their play instinct will not only make much more normal human beings but will also make better business men, better professional men, better citizens, better men and women generally. They will succeed better and have a nobler influence in the world. Joy and fun are great developers, calling out our richest resources, educating our finest powers.

It is self-expression that develops power along moral as well as mental and physical lines. If one is constantly repressed, his faculties will be stifled and his moral nature will also suffer. Repression causes arrested development in more children than almost anything else. There must be freedom, a sense of liberty for self-expression, otherwise the mind will not give up its best, the body will be stunted, and the whole being will be impoverished.

A poor boy who had been taken from the slums to a boys' farm home, and who had been told all his life that he was good-for-nothing, said to the other boys: "I dunno nothin' and I alius did. My parents alius tole me I wuz nobody and never would be."

Physicians tell us that the sexual plagues which curse so many youths are often due to lack of proper physical exercise and play. Boys like this little lad who have no boyhood, who are brought up to work, who have very little or no play in their lives, who do not have an outlet for their fun-loving propensities, are very much more apt to fall into vicious sexual habits than those who have plenty of wholesome exercise and fun.

There is nothing else so helpful to the normal development of the sexual life as a lot of play and fun and plenty of physical exercise of a vigorous sort, such as boxing, wrestling, football, baseball, rowing, running, etc. All these things are splendid for boys and give them a wholesome outlet for their energies, which is extremely important, especially between the ages of twelve and twenty.

Boys who have a great deal of healthful, wholesome exercise out of doors with good associates, boys who retire so healthily tired that they fall asleep almost as soon as their heads touch their pillows, and who are encouraged to rise immediately when they first awake are not likely to become victims of vicious habits.

When a youth has complete self-expression, when he has all the play and fun which his nature demands: when he runs and plays to his heart's content in the open air, there is little danger of pent-up longings and desires finding outlet in forbidden ways. But the moment he is suppressed, forbidden normal exercise out-of-doors and housed too closely, his abnormal appetites come into ascendency, and, not having been trained in self-mastery, he often becomes the prey of evil suggestions and temptations.

Pent-up desires and passions, like volcanoes, when they are stifled, will break out somewhere.

One reason why many youths go wrong is because they are not given sufficient outlet for their pent-up energies, their activities are limited. They have no proper childhood. They do not have enough fun, enough romance ; their homes are too serious.

Mothers are often terribly shocked by the development of what they regard as the sudden depravity of their daughters, who run away with men, or are otherwise led astray. They seem to think that the sudden lapse is quite unaccountable, but we notice that these things happen oftenest in straight-laced homes, where the girls have been over-chaperoned, over-protected, suppressed, repressed, and hedged in at every point. Such a life is not normal for healthy, active girls. Their boundless energies must have an outlet; and, if they are not allowed a natural one, they will force one in some unforeseen, unfortunate direction. If these girls had been given more freedom, if they had been thrown more upon their own responsibility, their good behavior, they would have developed more character, more will power, more common sense and moral fiber. It is a great injustice to a girl to bring her up in a glass case, shielded from every rough wind, not allowed any freedom of expression, to bring her up in such a way that she is likely to become an easy prey to evil masculine influences.

A girl should be so reared and trained as to be always strong and vigorous, self-reliant,] able to judge for herself, and to be independent] at all stages of her growth. The soft, flabby, characterless girl who has been over-protected and over-watched, when she attains her majority and a certain measure of liberty, is likely to do all sorts of hazardous things which may be fatal.

There is a happy medium in this matter of training children, as in everything else, which produces the best results. To give children too much liberty and freedom of action is as pernicious as to give them too little. The outcome is usually productive of as much evil in the one case as in the other.

It is imperative, however, that those who have the care and training of children should remember that there is a terrific force in youth which, if not directed into useful, helpful channels, becomes a menace. Many parents do not fully appreciate this tremendous pent-up energy in their children, nor realize that, unless there is a legitimate channel for its expression, it will find an illegitimate one.

Some over-strict fathers and mothers who manage to keep depraving influences away from their children by perpetually watching and chaperoning them make the mistake of starving their imaginations by suppressing their love of romance instead of guiding it into healthy channels.

There is a great deal of romance and love of adventure in all normal children, and, if this is suppressed, strangled, there is a corresponding deficiency in the nature. Any function which is not used atrophies, dries up, and we are so much the less natural.

Few parents realize what a powerful part romance plays in young lives. It is as natural for children to play, to dream, to romance, as it is for them to breathe. This is their normal expression.

It is astonishing how many youths, and even children among the poor, consult fortune tellers and palmists, many of whom are connected with disreputable houses. They predict riches, handsome husbands, and a luxurious life for pretty girls, and they often play into the hands of pals, who gradually ensnare the girls into evil ways.

A leader in settlement work tells of a hardworking girl who was told by a palmist that diamonds and all sorts of luxuries were coming to her soon. After this she accepted a diamond ring from a man whose improper attentions she had previously withstood.

In this way many ill-trained young girls, while searching for adventure and trying to satisfy their longing for romance, are led into a vicious life.

Regular habits, plenty of sleep,—outdoor sleeping rooms are the most healthful—fresh air, a happy home life,—home made so pleasant, harmonious and beautiful that children prefer it to any other place on earth— all these are tremendous influences in molding a pure, noble life. And such influences are very necessary to-day, for, at best our whole American life is dangerously stimulating and over-exciting for young people.

Owing to the fact that in the past boys were brought up with the idea that, while impurity in a girl was the unforgivable sin, for them it brought no punishment—was, indeed, by those who should guide them upward, considered necessary for their health—they now require especial care, even more than girls, during the dangerous years of adolescence.

For this reason changes in a growing boy should be watched very carefully. A youth who becomes shy and morose at this time, who secludes himself from the rest of the family, who always wants to be alone, and especially the one who has an unnatural appetite, is just the one to be watched and cautioned by parents or guardians.

The abuse of the sexual function has a peculiarly demoralizing, deteriorating influence upon the nervous system, upon the mental as well as the moral faculties. There is something so especially degrading in the perversion of the sexual instinct and functions that it coarsens the whole nature.

We are often shocked at the gradual change in the disposition and appearance of growing boys, whose entire being becomes coarse, repellent. Ignorant parents try to explain these radical changes in disposition and appearance, the gradual coarsening of their boys, by their rapid growth and development, when it is often in reality due to the perversion of the sexual functions, for it is certain that something fine and delicate and beautiful goes out of the life after any contamination of this nature.

Great care should be taken during this dangerous period to give the boy the right kind of food. Meats, condiments, rich sauces, all things which would arouse passion, especially at night, should be forbidden. All food should be avoided which tends to disturb the sleep, and the boy should be taught to jump out of bed in the morning the moment he wakes.

If all children were to eat their principal meal in the middle of the day, and to have a light supper, something like corn bread and milk, they would have sweet, refreshing sleep, free from the restlessness and irritation caused by rich foods, especially meats, with piquant sauces, condiments, etc. Rich, complex diets are not for youth, and parents little realize what risks they run in giving their children such food.

I know families where the children are not only allowed to eat heavy meats, gravies and all sorts of condiments for dinner, but they are also allowed to eat late at night, just before going to bed. These children are not only abnormally nervous and irritable, but their skin is covered with blotches. Then they are allowed to go to all sorts of places, theatres, dances, and other amusements late in the evening, and, as a rule, do not get to bed until after they should have had at least two or three hours' sound sleep. In short, their whole training is calculated to overdevelop the sexual instinct, to hasten instead of to retard the period of puberty.

The ignoring of the whole subject of sex by parents, their carelessness or ignorance in regard to the question of food, exercise, amusements, etc., for their children, especially during the years approaching puberty, has wrought much suffering and sorrow in the lives of millions of boys and girls.

Every healthy youth has a real ambition to win out in life, to make good, to stand for something. He may not realize just how he is going to do this, but he has a sort of general understanding with himself that he is going to be somebody, and if he fails to achieve his ambition there is something wrong in his training, something vicious in his environment.

Normal boys do not deliberately plan to form habits or to do things which are going to seriously cripple or absolutely defeat their ability to make good in the world. They form such habits and do such things ignorantly.

If you parents would help your boys to take account of their success and welfare assets, if you would explain to them that their capital lies in their health, and this in turn in their food, their exercise, their recreation, care of their body; if you would point out to them that their possibilities for making good in life consist in their courage, their ambition, their aspiration, their ideal, their determination, their persistent industry, their grit, their initiative, their self-reliance, and that all of these can be tremendously strengthened or impaired in the degree that they care for or neglect their health, you would find that no normal youth would deliberately throw away his precious life capital by succumbing to vicious habits. No well reared, properly instructed boy would insist upon wasting his vitality, squandering his precious life force in any form of debauchery.

As civilization advances, the struggle for life becomes more and more intense. As our material standards of living grow higher and higher, as comforts and luxuries increase, so do the perils and temptations that assail the higher spiritual life multiply. You do not know what dangers may beset your children when they leave the home nest to make their own way in the world.

As a matter of fact, one of the most dangerous periods in the lives of boys and girls is that between leaving school and getting employment; because, instead of having, as they should, when they leave school, a pretty good idea of what they are best fitted for, they blunder around, often for many months, perhaps years, before finding the place which is at all suited to them.

If the State afforded the children in all our schools proper vocational training, as it will someday, this interval would be greatly lessened. In the meantime, thousands of youths are led astray while waiting for work after leaving school. Having no special training, nor any idea what vocation they are best fitted to enter, they often experiment a long time before they get permanently located, and in this interval are frequently drawn into all sorts of vicious experiences, which lead to their ruin.

Questionable employments are also a moral menace to growing boys and girls. Only a few years ago the country was stirred up over the terrible revelations of the demoralizing influences to which messenger boys who are obliged to go on errands to disreputable houses at night are subjected. A great many fine youths are thus led into vice through familiarity with evil. Many business men who lead double lives employ them to carry their secret messages, flowers, and presents, to such places. Sometimes they are sent to the better parts of the city, apparently to reputable houses; but often they are called to the vilest resorts, and sent for liquors and drugs.

Although the telegraph companies have done a great deal to stop this evil, yet only a few states, for example. New York and Wisconsin, have raised the legal age of night messengers to twenty-one years.

I have known many cases where splendid boys who went into the messenger service during the Christmas holidays, or on special occasions, have been led into vicious practices by becoming familiar with evil when on errands which have taken them into disreputable places. They have been there brought in contact with a side of life of which they had known nothing previously, and, not having been safeguarded, forewarned, by their parents, who have always remained silent upon the sex question, they have become easy victims of vice and ignorance. If these boys had been properly trained, had been posted in these matters, and warned of the terrible possible results from sexual abuse or sin, they might have been spared their tragic experiences.

A noted settlement worker tells how many youths of good moral impulses have been led into vicious lives through the influence of liberal tips which they have received from inmates of disreputable houses. She says that they are often given fees of a dollar or more when they are sent to buy cocaine, morphine, or some other drug, or ice cream, cake, or sweetmeats. More than one messenger boy, through his familiarity with evil, has fallen so low as to become a white slave trader.

The majority of youths who become sexually tainted and wrecked get into the mire through sheer ignorance. They do not know what it means, just as most of the girls who go wrong do so because of their utter ignorance of it all. People do not voluntarily go into things which they know spell ruin. They simply do not know. They have not been properly trained.

5

WHITE SLAVERY AND THE CHILD WOMAN

We are very slightly changed From the semi-apes who ranged

India's prehistoric clay; Whoso drew the longest bow Ran his brother down, you know,

As we run men down to-day. —Kipling.

Kipling's famous stanza, given above, would be still more appropriate and forcible had he substituted for "men" in the last line the word women, meaning the women—the child-women especially—who are driven or beguiled into "white slavery."

"Suffer little children to come unto me, and forbid them not; for of such is the kingdom of God," said the Founder of Christianity two thousand years ago. In Chicago, New York, London, Paris, Berlin, and all the other great centres of the Christian world, we answer His invitation by suffering them to be swept into the brothels!

Of one hundred and thirty girls who had gone wrong in a certain district in Chicago, recent investigation revealed the fact that the majority of them had become victims of vice at the average age of eight!

Many of the children brought into the juvenile courts, and rescued by protective societies do not seem to realize what they are doing or what it must all lead to. On one occasion, when Jane Addams was asked to go to a rescue home and address the inmates, she tells how, when she got there, she found on the little white bed of every child or on the stiff white chair beside it, the dolls of the delinquent owners, still young enough to love those supreme toys of childhood! Her lecture, she said, did not fit the occasion, so she remained to dress dolls for a company of little girls, who eagerly asked her all about the dolls she possessed in her childhood!

In "A New Conscience and an Ancient Evil," the author gives an account of a little girl, the only child of a widowed mother, who sold newspapers in a disreputable neighborhood where dissolute people frequented the hotels. The child made a good deal of money and the poor mother thought she was too young to understand the vile things which she might see. But a little later she was horrified to find that her child was familiar with vice, and, eventually, the girl became an inmate of one of the resorts where she had so long sold papers and gum.

Another case cited is that of a woman who did a thriving business in a disreputable house, which was supplied largely by three or four little girls. They brought their girlfriends to the house, and became so hardened by the money and the little fineries, candies and presents they received that they did not seem to be seriously troubled when they knew that bringing their friends to this house would probably be their ruin.

This constitutes one of the most appalling phases of the White Slave traffic, the holocaust of child victims, who are ruined before they are old enough to know the nature of evil; who, before reason or education can let the light into their minds, become hardened and toughened into insensibility.

A physician connected with the New York Society for the Prevention of Cruelty to Children says it is horribly pathetic to learn how far a nickel or a quarter will go towards purchasing the virtue of young girls. In investigations of vice in New York it was found that a great many girls have been lured to pay for a merry-go-round ride, or admission to some picture show, with the price of their chastity!

The vilest of men give young girls pennies and nickels on the street, and in business places, in order to become acquainted with them, to gain their confidence, and just these little things are the entering wedges to their ruin.

It is unfortunate that many poor parents not only do not try to discourage their children from accepting money, or tickets for places of amusement, from strangers; but, when the children come home and tell them that a nice man gave them a ride on a hobby horse or on a merry-go-round, or gave them a ticket to a picture show, they seem to think that it is so much gained, that their children are fortunate in getting these things free. They do not realize the danger lurking in those seemingly innocent gifts.

The vile men who lead innocent children astray know very well that there is nothing else they love so much as fun and adventure; that they will do all sorts of things for a good time. Children's curiosity is very strong, and, their self-control being weak, they will go to almost unbelievable lengths to satisfy it. They want to see things; they want to have experiences, and the agents of vice take advantage of this to exploit them. A child is a bundle of sensitive nerves athrill with the desire to see and to know, to play.

Those who are lured by the promise of a little fun may have very little sunshine in their lives. Their surroundings may be discordant, vulgar and indecent. An intemperate father may make their so-called home a hell on earth. They may really have no normal home life, may know little of love or affection, may have little or no outlet for their pent-up, fun-loving, romance-craving energies.

Is it strange that poor children, who seldom have a penny or a nickel of their own to spend as they please, should be lured into all sorts of places of amusement by free tickets? How often I have seen poor little ones standing about a merry-go-round, longing for a ride, a treat which, perhaps, they have never had in all their young lives. How they envy the more fortunate children! How little they dream of evil in the kind stranger who offers to gratify their longing!

City children are often allowed to go into disreputable houses to sell papers and gum to the inmates, who are usually liberal to them, often declining to take change; and the parents, in many cases, are so greedy to get the money which they bring home that they do not make proper efforts to keep them out of such places. Indeed, in some cities, even when the police have tried to protect them, the children actually have had special permits from the mayors, in response to appealing letters from the parents, pleading their great poverty, as an excuse for begging the special privilege of allowing their little ones to sell their wares in those dangerous houses.

It is a disgrace to our civilization that innocent children should be so exposed to evil that in a multitude of cases they are almost sure of being led astray.

Isn't it a shame that, in this land of opportunity where there should be a fair chance and plenty for every human being, vast multitudes of innocent children should be forced to live under conditions which are not fit for any human beings, which would be a severe test of the virtue and morality of grown men and women of clean, pure lives!

Think of the tremendous danger to purity in the crowded, so-called homes of the poor, where often entire families are obliged to live in one or two rooms, where the sanitary conditions are most demoralizing, destructive alike to moral and physical health! Think of those foul tenement houses and underground cellars where the sun never enters, where the old and young of both sexes are thrown together without any distinction; where very often poor parents take into, it may be, one room where there are already several children, a boarder or two to help pay the rent; and then let us ask ourselves. Is it any wonder that under such circumstances the natural safeguards of reserve and modesty break down? Is it any wonder that with such conditions in the home, added to constant familiarity with vice and crime in their general environment, multitudes of children drift into disreputable careers?

We call this a land of equal opportunity.

But do those children, who are obliged to live in the very midst of vice during their most impressionable years, when every sight, every sound, every experience, is indelibly photographed upon the growing brain, have a fair chance in life? Are those children who grow up to maturity with their minds saturated with impure experiences; who live in an atmosphere of vice; for whom evil is robbed of its hideous-ness by constant familiarity; who are reared with the idea that profanity, obscenity and sexual sin are not very bad, because "everybody does it,"—are those children responsible for their ultimate degradation and ruin?

Just think, you well-to-do parents, if, under the most favorable conditions, where you can control the environment of your children and give them all the rights of childhood, many of you have such a struggle with them during the dangerous years when they are approaching and passing through puberty, what it must mean at this critical period for those other children who are struggling with their awakening passions amid associations which tend to arouse, to inflame the lowest animal instincts! Think what it must mean to be constantly in an atmosphere where morbid imaginings are aroused by vile insinuations, the most vulgar allusions, sights, and suggestive experiences, in an environment where impurity is the rule of life! What are the chances for their surviving years of such experiences and coming out clean, pure, and wholesome; when, perhaps, with all your care and the constant suggestion of purity and wholesome home environment, you may not be able to protect your own child from sexual defilement or degeneracy?

Thousands of respectable, hard-working fathers and mothers with large families, living in cities, and earning small wages, must look for the cheapest possible rent, which is often found next to a saloon or near a disorderly house or a dance hall. How are those parents going to protect their young boys and girls from the dangers that surround them in such a neighborhood?

In such poor homes too, there are no provisions for personal cleanliness, for taking a bath; and uncleanliness is a factor in developing impurity. Yet many of the children in those homes grow up almost without knowing what a real, thorough bath means. Absolute cleanliness of person;

clean, wholesome, hygienic surroundings; plenty of healthful exercise, physical and mental; a lot of innocent play and wholesome fun,—these are things which tend to keep the mind pure. What chance have the children of the slums for getting them?

Again, thousands of poor mothers are obliged to go out to work in the daytime, and must leave their little ones exposed to all the vile influences at work in their poverty-stricken neighborhood during their absence. The loss of the mother's care, especially when she is in-Telligent and has been well trained, is a very great factor in children going to the bad; for, while there are many exceptions, it is the rule that neglected children who grow up in the midst of temptation and are familiar with evil are, in the end, likely to become victims of their environment.

"I can recall a very intelligent woman," says Jane Addams, "who long brought her children to the Hull House day nursery. The little girl is almost totally deaf, owing to neglect following a case of measles, when her mother could not stop work in order to care for her; the youngest boy has lost a leg flipping cars; the oldest has twice been arrested for petty larceny; the twin boys, in spite of prolonged sojourns in the truant school, have been such habitual truants that their natural intelligence has secured but little aid from education. Of the five children three now are in semi-penal institutions supported by the State. It would not, therefore," she added, "have been so uneconomical to have boarded them with their own mother, requiring a standard of nutrition and school attendance at least up to the national standard of nurture which the more advanced European governments are establishing."

When will our country, which boasts of its equal opportunities, free its mothers from the slavery of poverty and allow them to care for their own children, to rear them in hygienic, sanitary and moral decency?

Think of allowing a mother to work out for fifty cents a day, when her influence upon her children during that time, even measured solely by its economic value to the State, bears no legitimate comparison to the wretched pittance she earns!

Just imagine, you happy, well-to-do parents, what these poor mothers, who work themselves to death for their children, suffer when they feel that, in spite of all their efforts and sacrifices, their little ones are slipping away because of the evil associations and vicious influences brought to bear upon them during their enforced absence!

The time will come when the State will find that it is at a perilous cost that it allows mothers to bring up children during their spare time, in the evenings, at night, after they have done hard days' work washing and scrubbing, or after toiling long hours in factories. It will find that it does not pay to allow women who are sacrificing their lives for their children to be compelled to leave them to chance during the daytime, while they are obliged for a ridiculous compensation to do that for which they are, perhaps, totally unfitted, thus robbing their little ones of that mother-love and mother-influence which would tend to shape their lives into usefulness, and make them good citizens. What a tragedy, what a reflection upon our civilization, that such things are necessary!

"Save the children and you save the nation," said Marcus M. Marks, borough president of Manhattan, in a speech at the opening of a Hebrew kindergarten and day nursery in New York City. "Philanthropy for the benefit of the old serves individuals only, but work for the young affects generations yet unborn."

That is the crux of this whole question: in caring for the children of to-day we are insuring well-born children in the future, the advancement of the whole race. As Rabbi M. Hyamson of London, said in speaking of similar work in England, "The work of day nurseries provides for better children of the future as well as for better children in the present."

"If children are not brought up well," said ex-President Roosevelt, "they are not merely a curse to themselves, but they mean the ruin of the State in the future."

Some time ago scientists traced the cost to the State of New York of the descendants of a single criminal woman, made so largely through neglect, insufficient nourishment and lack of training in childhood. There were thousands of these degenerate descendants, and their crimes, trials, and penitentiary expenses have cost the State over a million dollars.

A comparatively few dollars in the proper training of the ancestors of these costly criminals might have saved all this.

It is possible not only to save young lives from the horrors and evils of impurity, but pretty nearly all the crime with its awful cost and demoralization to the community could be prevented if we would only take the children in charge, and insist at the outset upon a healthful rearing, proper hygienic environment, proper playgrounds, proper recreation and chaperonage during their minority. The demoralization of children takes place within a comparatively few years when they are very impressionable, at an age when they ought to have and are entitled to have the best possible training.

When we remember that the minds of children are like the sensitive plates of a photographer, recording every thought or suggestion to which they are exposed, we must realize how important it is that they should hear and see only that which will make for nobility of character, for beauty, and for truth. It is the things that are seen and heard and learned in childhood that make up the character and determine the future possibilities of the man and woman.

Think of a child reared in the contaminating atmosphere of the slums of a great city where everything is dripping with suggestions of vulgarity and wickedness of every description! Think of its young mind being constantly filled with profanity, obscenity, and filth! Think of what it hears and sees, what it has indelibly impressed on its plastic imagination every day, every hour of its young life! Then contrast such a child with one that is brought up in an atmosphere of purity, refinement, and culture; whose mind is continually filled with noble, uplifting suggestions of the true, the pure, and the beautiful! What a difference in the fate of the two children, and without any effort or choice whatever of their own! One mind is trained downward, toward darkness; the other, upward, toward the light. What chance has the first to develop a noble character when all of its first impressionable years are saturated with the suggestions of evil with which its environment reeks, when quarreling, bickering, foul language, indecency,—all that is low and degrading continually fills its ears and eyes?

How long will we suffer children to be brought up under such conditions and then punish them when they develop into crooks and criminals? How long will the State continue to build prisons and asylums for degenerates, to expend far more money in housing and feeding the criminal classes than would be required to save the children before they become degenerate?

There are, it is true, signs of an awakening. The women's movement is making itself felt in this, as in all other great questions looking toward the uplift of mankind. Their activities in behalf of women and children are arousing legislatures all over the country. The State is beginning to discover that the children are her greatest asset, which she cannot afford to waste through neglect, or bad rearing on the part of unfortunate or degenerate parents. She realizes that something must be done to chaperone or properly mother all her neglected children during the perilous years when their self-control is undeveloped and their passions insistent and imperative, instead of letting them go to the bad.

Neither the State nor the individual, not one of us can shirk our share of responsibility for the terrible sacrifice of innocent children to the evils in our midst, especially to that most terrible of all human ills—white slavery.

6
HOW THE SLAVE MART IS SUPPLIED

Is there, in human form, that bears a heart,—

A wretch! a villain! lost to love and truth! That can, with studied, sly, ensnaring art,

Betray sweet Jenny's unsuspecting youth? Curse on his perjured arts, dissembling smooth!

Are honor, virtue, conscience, all exiled? Is there no pity, no relenting ruth.

Points to the parents fondling o'er their child. Then paints the ruined maid, and their distraction wild?

— Robert Burns.

Neither man nor angel can discern Hypocrisy, the only evil that walks Invisible, except to God alone. By his permissive will, through heaven and earth.

— John Milton.

In response to the demand that the "social evil," or to give it its proper name, prostitution, be legalized in our country and its victims licensed. Dr. Howard Kelly, in a vigorous protest, said; "Where shall we look to recruit the ever-failing ranks of these poor creatures as they die yearly by tens of thousands ? Which of the little girls of our land shall we designate for this traffic? Mark their sweet innocence to-day as they run about in our streets and parks, prattling and playing, ever busy about nothing; which of them shall we snatch as they approach maturity, to supply this foul mart?"

Think of the greatest nations in the world, England, France, Germany, and other European countries protecting or legalizing this infamous traffic in the bodies and souls of women under the plea that it is necessary for the well-being of men!

For centuries English government authorities have sanctioned the "social evil" in the army and navy, and have established measures to protect the health of the soldiers and sailors; but they have felt no concern whatever about the fate of the women sacrificed to the system. "The government," says an authoritative writer on the subject, "is directly responsible for a large measure of white slavery. It is, in effect, a procurer of women for the vicious pleasures of men in the army and navy. . . .

"Many of the white slaves of these brothels [in British India] sanctioned and supervised by the government are, it is said, mere children.

How are they obtained, and what happens to them when they become hopelessly diseased and thus misfit for use by the officers and soldiers'?"

When the English opponents of this awful prostitution of the power of the State made their great fight to induce the government to repeal the terrible Contagious Disease Act relating to the garrison towns of Great Britain, where it permitted and legalized sexual vice, they were subjected to all sorts of insults and abuse for meddling with a custom which had been entrenched in military camps for generations !

We have broken away from many of the harmless customs and traditions of the mother country. Isn't it time that we broke away from a vile precedent like this?

Our civilization is responsible for the great moral evil. There was no such thing as prostitution among the primitive tribes, and it is unknown in the hot climates where people go practically naked. The mystery with which we surround sex and the morbid curiosity aroused by the suggestion of dress seem to play no inconsiderable part in the perversion of the grandest, the sublimest human instinct; that instinct which, when properly used and kept clean and pure, blossoms out into beauty, into all that is most healthful and noble in life, but which, when abused, misused, perverted, leads to the greatest degradation of which human beings are capable.

But the civilized governments of the world which either legalize and sanction vice or wink at it and encourage it in their young men, are responsible for many of its worst phases to-day.

Dr. Martindale, author of "Under the Surface," quotes a British ex-official who for many years had charge of the government brothels, or chaklas, as they are called in India, as follows :— "I cannot speak too strongly against them. Many a young boy or man comes out to India pure and good. It is the presence of the government chaklas that first put it into his head to lead a vicious life. Many resist for a time, but when they see their friends and their superior officers making use of them, and when they are given to understand that the medical inspection makes it safe for them to go to them, sooner or later they give way and follow the example of the rest.

But to start with, — they don't want to"

Think of a great Christian government actually seducing its young men! Is it any wonder that the evil flourishes in India, in England, and in our own country, where, if it is not legalized, procurers, debauchers of both young men and young women are so lightly dealt with!

"Be not afraid of them that kill the body, and after that have no more that they can do," said Christ to his apostles; "but I will forewarn you whom ye shall fear. Fear him who after he hath killed hath power to cast into hell; yea, I say unto you, fear him."

But in Christian America the man who kills the body is electrocuted, while those who make a business of killing the souls of young girls are practically immune from any punishment.

During the recent exposure of the white slave traffic in New York City, it was found that the men who live in luxury from the profits of women's ruin and degradation have a regular systematized plan for securing "new material."

They ply their vile business even at the very doors of our schoolhouses. "Cadets," as the male procurers are called, hang around the schools at the time of closing and try to flirt with the more attractive girls, who are flattered by the notice of these young men, who often dress in the height of fashion. In many cases they get into conversation with the schoolgirls, give them cards and invite them to call at their apartments, or they invite them to the theatre, to picture shows, to automobile rides, to dinner in some fashionable place, where they often induce them to drink and thus get them in their power.

A clergyman in New York reports a typical case where one of those "cadets" inveigled two schoolgirls to visit his apartment, and it was found that they had been going there regularly for some time when their parents discovered it.

After a girl has once yielded to the temptation to do an imprudent thing, her pride keeps her from making a confidant of her mother or anyone else; and the fascination, the exhilaration of the new experience, arouses her curiosity and the desire to repeat it until the first thing she knows she is charmed beyond her own control, and led to her ruin.

In many instances it is the girl's very innocence and her love of romance that are her undoing; the fact that she is unsophisticated, and does not know that these men are experts in their vile trade, hypnotizing and fascinating girls just as serpents charm birds until they drop off from the trees. Sometimes "cadets" will work on an attractive girl for months before they "land" her, as they say, because they know that she is valuable in proportion to her attractiveness.

It is well known that in our large cities certain low theatrical agencies are in league with disreputable houses. A prominent social worker tells the story of two fine young English girls, one sixteen, the other seventeen, who had gained extraordinary skill in juggling, and who came to this country under an agreement with a theatrical manager to pay them five shillings ($1.25) a week and their expenses. This manager became stranded in the West, and the girls were turned loose. They applied to a theatrical agency in Chicago for positions, and were sent to a disreputable house where a vaudeville programme was given every night. They took the position in good faith, not knowing, of course, the character of the house. When they did realize the nature of the place they became frightened and managed to escape from the dressing room while they were awaiting their turn to go on the stage. They got out on the street and appealed to policemen for protection. They were sent to the Juvenile Protective Association.

Many unprincipled agents bring colored girls to our Northern cities from the South. They sometimes pay the girls' fares, and, if they do not succeed in getting good situations immediately, so that they can return the money advanced to them—often an exorbitant sum,— they are sent as waitresses and chambermaids to disreputable houses. They are ignorant of the character of these places until, perhaps, it is too late for them to protest; and even if they do, they may be forced to remain there under threats of police intervention or of personal violence until they can pay back the money. In the meantime the girls grow so accustomed to their vile surroundings that their hideous-ness gradually diminishes, their sensibilities become hardened, and they often enter the life themselves. Unscrupulous employment bureaus often send colored girls to disreputable houses when they would not dare so to treat white girls.

One reason why so many colored girls go wrong is because they are only a few generations removed from slavery, in which state no regard was paid to their sex. It has only been a short time since they began to exercise their self-control. They have had comparatively little responsibility along the line of legitimate motherhood. When we remember their many generations of bondage, their necessarily unstable marriage and parental relations, the frightfully illicit example their slave masters set them, the fact that they are still looked upon as an inferior race, and that they are usually poor and live in depraved neighborhoods, where the children are an easy prey to demoralizing influences, it is quite remarkable that, as a whole, the colored people are as moral, as conscientious as they are to-day.

A large proportion of the victims of white slavery are from farms and smaller towns in the country. They are more easily duped by the wiles of the procurers than city girls, and their identity is more easily hidden; besides they are more readily controlled, because they do not know much about city life. Many of these young girls are led to their doom in just trying to see what the world is like. They have been kept close to the home and know almost nothing of life. When they get away and get a little more liberty, love of romance and adventure and their ignorance lead them astray.

These girls from the country never have been taught that a young girl, friendless and alone in a large city, is in greater danger than she would be alone with the wild beasts in the jungles of Africa; that thousands of men are watching for just such girls as they, waiting to lure them to their ruin, setting all sorts of traps for them. They are never told, perhaps, that thirty thousand men in New York City alone, not to speak of Chicago, Boston, St. Louis, and other big centres, make it a profession to lure just such innocent young girls into sin, and that many of them become rich in this awful traffic in human lives.

The country girl who has been accustomed to a quiet, simple life is often thrown off her guard by the glitter of the city, the evidences of luxurious living,—beautiful dresses, fine automobiles, and people everywhere on pleasure bent. She is dazzled by these things and often loses her mental balance.

Such an unsophisticated, inexperienced girl is easily enticed to public dance halls, where young men who are experts in misleading girls often induce her to drink, and the proprietor purposely makes it very difficult to get water in these places. The dances last only four or five minutes, because the chief aim of the halls is to get the inmates to buy drinks. Thousands of girls are thus induced to drink, and, before they realize it, the hour is late and the young men persuade them that they cannot afford to go home, but that they can explain the next morning that they stayed with their friends.

In other words, the most damnable methods are used to play upon the credulity and the vanity of these young girls. As a rule, of course, the girls know nothing about the character of the men who are trying to ruin them; who tell them, especially if they are attractive, that it is a shame that such handsome girls should not have diamonds and beautiful clothes, and thus play upon their vanity. They often make them behave that they can get places for them on the vaudeville or theatrical stage, and that they will introduce them to managers, etc. These bogus managers are in the game with the "cadets," and, under the pretense of helping the girls to positions, lead them farther and farther to their ruin.

There are six hundred public dance halls in Chicago, and probably more than a thousand in New York. The majority of them are connected directly with saloons, and in all of them liquors are sold. Bad men feel pretty sure of a girl if they can persuade her to take a drink, and the fact that the girls go to the dance halls when weary after a hard day's work, makes it all the easier for them to be induced to do so on the plea that a drink will brace them up.

Drugs and alcohol are the most potent aids of the white slave traffic. Many of its victims say that they could not endure their horrible life without the deadening influence of alcohol, opium, or cocaine.

"Whoever has tried to help a girl who is making an effort to leave the irregular life she has led," said Jane Addams, "must have been discouraged by the victim's attempts to overcome using alcohol and drugs. Such a girl has commonly been drawn into this life in the first place when under the influence of liquor, and has continued to drink that she might be able to live through each day. The drink habit grows upon her, for she is constantly required to sell liquors and to be treated."

When General Bingham was police commissioner of New York, he said, "There is not enough depravity in human nature to keep alive this very large business. The immorality of women and the brutishness of men have to be persuaded, coaxed and constantly stimulated in order to keep the social evil in its present state of prosperity."

If the Government should prohibit the sale of liquors in disreputable houses, sever all connection between the saloon, the dance hall and these places of vice, severely punish proprietors of disreputable houses whenever liquor was found on the premises, sold or brought there, it would be a tremendous blow to the worst traffic that ever cursed the earth.

The whole white slave business has been forced because it was found profitable. Men who are mean and stingy in their homes, are liberal and even reckless in their expenditures on vice. When a man's senses are deadened with drink, and his mind sodden with bestial orgies, money does not mean much to him. This is where the unfortunates who have been ruined endeavor to be revenged on the men who first led them astray. They ply them with drink and force their bestiality in every possible way, to increase their income. This fact, together with the twenty-five per cent, profit on every drop of liquor sold, makes alcohol the greatest asset in the white slave trade.

The most hopeless thing in the underworld is the sordid love of money, the selfish desire for a life of ease, which tempts so many young-men to make a profession of exploiting white slaves. When, moreover, one young man makes a success of ruining fellow beings, his associates find it out and each one thinks there is an opportunity for him also to make an easy living in the same way. Greed and selfishness so grow upon these men in their demoralizing traffic that they become inhumanly cruel.

Many of the wretched white slaves support in luxury and idleness the men who have ruined them, and these very men whom they thus support by the profits of their shame often treat them most brutally, driving them out into the night in all sorts of weather, and snatching from them nearly every penny of their miserable earnings on their return.

Not long ago a girl was found in a vicious resort in New York who was so far gone with tuberculosis that she was subject to severe hemorrhages; and, because she refused to go out in the cold and storm, her slave owner was seen to strike her in the face as she was having a bad coughing spasm. At one o'clock in the morning he pushed her out of the door into the street, telling her that if she did not bring him money before morning he would renounce his police protection and she should go to prison.

Think of such damnable business being carried on right under our noses in what we call one of the most civilized cities in the world! African slavery was a race blessing in comparison with this nefarious trade!

The procurers in many cases are protected by the police, and the girls are kept in constant horror lest their masters withdraw their protection and turn them over to the police for arrest and imprisonment. Fear is the club held over tens of thousands of these unfortunates.

The young men in this wretched business are usually well dressed and spend their money freely. They say that they live in the better part of the city and belong to good families, and will often tell girls they are trying to entrap that their parents want them to marry rich society girls, but that they would very much rather marry girls who work for a living, who do not put on so many airs. Many are thus lured into slavery by these men making love to them and pretending that they want to marry them. The girls become infatuated, and the young men deceive them.

Very few women would ever go wrong because of their animality alone.

It is her tender side, her gentle, romantic side which makes woman the easy victim of a scoundrel. He plays upon her most sacred instincts,—her maternal instinct, her longing for a home, her yearning for affection. These, and not passion, are the chief assets upon which the procurer plies his damnable trade. It is woman's tenderest feelings that oftenest lead to her downfall.

>Such is the fate of artless maid.
>
>Sweet floweret of the rural shade!
>
>By love's simplicity betrayed,
>
>And guileless trust.
>
>Till she, like thee, all soiled, is laid
>
>Low the dust. — Robert Burns. — "To a Mountain Daisy."

7

SMUGGLING POISONED GOODS

Gracious gods, grant that I may be beautiful within. — Socrates.

He that has light within his own clear breast May sit the centre, and enjoy bright day. — John Milton.

It has been said that great writers are usually distinguished by their power of setting the reader's mind to the active making of images. This is also unfortunately true of a class of writers who have no just claim to greatness, whose pernicious productions have done more to debauch the imagination of young people than any other one thing.

The most dangerous writers in the English language are those whose artful insinuations and mischievous polish reflect upon the mind the image of impurity without presenting the impurity itself. A plain vulgarity in a writer is its own antidote. It is like a foe who attacks us openly and gives us opportunity for defense. But impurity, secreted under beauty, under seductive attractiveness, is like a treacherous friend who strolls with us in a garden and destroys us by the odor of poisonous flowers proffered to our senses.

If the writers of suggestive fiction, fiction that presents the allurement of sex veiled in language none of whose words are actually impure, could see the miserable human wrecks they have made, the multitudes of splendid girls they have through their pages lured to their doom, the splendid young men whom they have led to sexual abuse, self-defilement, and all other sorts of sexual sin, if they did not drop dead from heart failure at the tragic sight, they would, at least, exile themselves to some distant place where they never again could look upon those whom they have ruined.

There is another class of writers exploiting the sex question who seem to think it necessary to open up sewers and uncover filthy places in order to show that they are unsanitary and dangerous. Some of these people are taking, advantage of the movement towards a higher morality to give the world needless descriptions and portrayals of places where so many youths are ruined. They are presenting vivid and wholly unnecessary pictures of the interiors of brothels and gambling dens, thus doing much harm instead of good. They seem to think that following these lurid descriptions with a few moral precepts will excuse the indecent temptations and evil suggestions which they drag into their writings. They do not try to give the young a clean, sweet, wholesome idea of the relation of sexes, but go just as near the illicit, the forbidden as possible, while still evading the law for circulation purposes. Like some French writers, they go just as near the indecent as possible without actually crossing the lines that would bar them from publication or circulation through the mails. Many of them have a wonderful art of insinuating and suggesting vicious pictures and situations which they do not actually express in words, and this suggestion of the vile is infinitely worse than the expression of it, because it stimulates an unwholesome curiosity and feeds a morbid imagination.

A very sensible woman, recently speaking of immoral filth of this sort which has passed our censors of morals and appeared not only in books, but also in some of our periodicals, indignantly declared that it was simply "smuggling poison past the guards."

Unfortunately much of this immoral suggestion of unscrupulous writers is smuggled into homes and finds its way to library shelves, and thus the printed page becomes the most subtle menace to the unformed minds, the vivid, questioning imaginations of the young.

Many playwrights and theatre managers, as well as writers of fiction and magazine articles, are also finding it very profitable to cater to morbid sexual desires. The same tendency visible in the worst forms of literature is seen in some of our theatres and moving picture shows. Playwrights and managers are presenting questionable plays, that just escape being illegal; plays that are pernicious enemies of society and lead to infinite harm. Their authors try to justify the dragging of this moral filth before the public by super-adding a moral emphasizing the necessity for better sex education.

The same is true of suggestiveness in art. Many impure artists have made their fortunes and their reputations, such as they were or are, upon forbidden ground, going just as near the point of legal prohibition as possible.

All these things have a most vicious influence upon the nervous system and the morals of growing youth, and parents should do everything in their power to counteract it. They should not only censor the plays and amusement places which their children attend, but also the books which they read and the sensual scandal-mongering newspapers with their nauseating details of divorce trials, murders, suicides, and general criminal records, which so many young boys and girls devour with avidity.

It is a thousand pities that the tragedies wrought by impure literature, vile pictures, and suggestive plays could not be brought home to their writers and producers, who should be scourged in public, and ever after ostracized by all decent people.

"Keep the imagination clean," said Hawthorne ; "that is one of the truest conditions of communion with heaven."

Mrs. Arthur Macy, who has been eyes, ears, and hands for Helen Keller during all her

years of training, says that, in one way at least, her blindness has been a good thing for this wonderful girl, because it has shut her out from the world of newspaper trash, the temptation to read the cheap, flippant, senseless articles in poor periodicals, and the great mass of vicious books and silly superficial "literature" with which the press is nowadays flooded. Owing to her afflictions, all of her reading has been most carefully selected. Her time has been too valuable to be worse than wasted in reading questionable novels, those which dwell upon topics of impurity and immorality. Her mind has never been tainted by impure suggestions or attractive pictures of evil. Her imagination has been kept wonderfully pure and clean by the constant inspiration of high ideals. Her acquaintances in literature have been of the highest type of authors, the most instructive, helpful, and uplifting. She has been spared the frightful blight of the sexual taint, which poisons the ears, the eyes, and the minds of so many young people to-day.

Childhood is the story age of life. The mind of a growing child delights in pure romance, and too much care cannot be exercised in the selection of its literature. The story-telling movement in our city libraries is one of the most admirable in our educational system. It introduces children to the world's masterpieces in literature and holds up for their example the highest ideals of life and conduct. If all parents had the time and the culture necessary to have a story hour for their children, there could be no better means of training their young imaginations or of impressing their minds with pure and lofty ideals.

Whatever else you do, don't allow your children to read exciting, trashy novels, blood-and-thunder stories, or cheap suggestive fiction, or to attend low picture shows or questionable plays. Boys especially should not be allowed to go to amusements which would tend to inflame the imagination. There are many vaudeville entertainments and picture shows that have a most unfortunate effect upon the boyish imagination. People little realize what they are doing when they allow their children, boys or girls, to see all sorts of plays and attend dances, where they are up late at night, and to do many other things in which not even adults can safely indulge.

If, where parents are indifferent, ignorant, or not adequate to do so, the State could properly supervise its youthful wards through the dangerous years of adolescence and keep away from them filthy, vulgar conversation, obscene pictures, and books frankly impure, even though they do not contain an improper word, that inflame the imagination, the morals of our people would be immeasurably raised; impurity would be largely stamped out.

If young people only realized what a terrible thing it is to get even a suggestion of impurity into the mind, they would never read an author whose lines drip with the very gall of death, or look at a picture that suggests evil.

One of the strangest things in human experience is the persistence, the insistence, the indelibility of bad things. Vicious stories, indelicate, vulgar jokes, impure suggestions, will pass over a whole continent and cross oceans, when a good thing, that which would inspire and uplift men, would travel at a snail's pace. Scandal will spread over a community like wildfire, whereas the good things said about our neighbors travel very slowly.

It is said that the mind's phonograph will faithfully reproduce a bad or impure story even up to the point of death. Many of our bishops and prominent clergymen have testified to the fact that the vicious things which they saw and heard back in their childhood come to them with all their original vividness in their most holy moments, when at their devotions and even when preaching funeral services. A distinguished preacher told me that an impure book was shown him when a boy, and that, although he had it in his sight but a few moments, he would, in after life, have parted with his right hand, if by so doing he could have blotted out its influence from his mind.

The great artist, Sir Peter Lely, refused to look upon a bad or inferior picture, because he declared that it would affect his standards and mar his ideals.

"I'd give my right hand," says John G. Gough, "if I could forget that which I have learned from impure associates, if I could tear from my brains the scenes which I have witnessed, the transactions which have taken place before me."

The tenacity, the indelibility of impure things no one yet has been able to explain, and for this reason it means everything to the future of boys and girls to keep such things out of their minds, to forbid their entrance,—to avoid impurity in every form.

A mayor of Philadelphia said he could rid the jails of two-thirds of the boy criminals in the next year if he could banish bad plays from the boards of the variety theatres and put bad books out of print. An officer of the British government declares that nearly all the boys brought before the criminal courts owe their downfall to impure reading.

It is probable that the careers of nearly every criminal in our prisons to-day would have been entirely different if the character of their reading when young had been different. It is impossible to estimate the damage which results from the poisoning of the mind in youth by vicious books or the suggestion of any form of impurity stamped upon the plastic brain.

Wounds of the body are nothing in comparison with wounds of the imagination which are rarely entirely healed. Physical mutilation is a boon compared with mutilation of the imagination. The hideous images, the vicious suggestions which come from a bad book, a bad picture, or a bad play, if they do not cripple or mar our career, may torment and haunt us all through life. Religion itself, the constant practice of virtue, cannot erase impure pictures indelibly imprinted on the youthful imagination.

A story is told of an archbishop of London who in his youth had his curiosity aroused to see some immoral, unsightly picture which was being displayed among his youthful companions. Many years after, when raised to the archbishopric, he was one day giving a sermon on "Purity," and this vile picture which he had looked upon in his college days would constantly come up in his mind to torment him and call him a hypocrite. He bitterly deplored his boyish curiosity and vainly wished that he had then possessed the knowledge of his later life, which would have made him immune to the temptation to look at any immoral thing.

One glance at a vulgar, indecent picture will make an unfading impression on the mind; the Life purpose may be changed, the outlook transformed, the aim completely reversed, but the hideous images and vile suggestions which were allowed to creep into the young life still persist in old age. They drag their foul presence into the most sacred experiences of life. They survive the years without a loss of tint or vividness, or of a shade of vile suggestiveness. They survive in the memory when ten thousand useful things have faded away,—even when a large part of our education has been forgotten. These enemies of purity seem to defy everything holy in life.

Chemists tell us that scarlet is the only color which cannot be bleached.

There is no known chemical which can remove it. So, when the sacred writer wished to emphasize the power of divine forgiveness, of divine love, he said: "Even though thy sins be as scarlet, they shall be made white as wool!" It takes omnipotent power to expunge impurity from the mind. Only divine love itself can bleach out of the character the sin of impurity.

Yet many people, and, I am sorry to say, among them clergymen, think that they must see evil, that they must visit questionable places, that they must go into the vile dens of the cities, into the houses of immorality, in order to see for themselves the hideousness of vice so that they may know how to rebuke and correct it.

There are multitudes who are very particular about the scrupulous cleanliness of their bodies, who could not be induced to miss their morning bath, but who wallow in mental sensuality, who indulge in perpetual debauches, in visualizing sin, and who never take a mental purity bath. Those people outwardly live moral lives; they do not drink nor visit immoral resorts, nor indulge in profane language, nor overstep the limits of propriety in any direction, but they live in perpetual mental sin. They are physically moral, extremely fastidious about their bodies, but they feed their minds upon the grossest pictures and plays, the filthiest literature they can get hold of. They do not realize that it is a thousand times worse to take filth into the mind than to take it into the body. Physical filth is nothing compared with mental and moral filth, taking into the mind the leaven of impurity.

As a matter of fact there is a direct connection between purity of mind and health of body. Moral filth is abnormal; it poisons and demoralizes the physical as well as the mental being, the body as well as the mind.

The blood cannot be kept clean and pure unless the thought is kept clean and pure. If the mind is saturated with uncleanness, if there is forbidden picturing constantly going on in the imagination, the blood will become vitiated. No one can ever estimate the fearful blight with which a perverted and diseased mentality will curse the entire life.

The imagination may be a source of vilest contagion. Keep it sane, pure, and wholesome, and you will have taken the most important step in building a noble character. I have found that impure stories, evil suggestions, indecent pictures, and the vulgar innuendoes of the impure minded are repulsive to children who have been intelligently and carefully educated regarding sex matters. Every child should be so trained against impurity, vulgarity, and every suggestion of obscenity that these things, instead of attracting, will disgust him, so that he will be immune from contaminating suggestion in whatever form it may be presented to him.

It is a most dangerous and cruel thing to keep pernicious literature in the home, within reach of growing boys or girls. It may make all the difference in their lives between purity and impurity, between happiness and misery.

We can hardly realize what a clean imagination in youth means, or how it will affect the whole career. The character and success of many a man would be very materially marred, if we were to eliminate from his life the great inspiring books he has read. Who, for instance, could tell what his life and character, and the history of this country would have been had Lincoln read dime novels and yellow-covered literature in his boyhood instead of the Bible, Plutarch's Lives, the biographies of great men like Washington and Franklin, Aesop's Fables, Robinson Crusoe and other inspirational and character-forming works?

It is a calamity that so much of our modem literature should appeal to the morbid, the impure in human nature, instead of the pure, the good; that writers should dwell upon the lowest rather than the highest elements in our nature. The constant suggestion of the good, the pure, the noble, the true, the awakening of the higher, the divine qualities in man, would revolutionize the mental attitude, the health, and the morals of the race.

If our dramatists would dwell less upon the abnormal and the vicious side of human nature ; if they would picture less of the bad and more of the good; if they would emphasize wickedness, immorality, vice, and the sins of humanity less, and goodness, morality, virtue, and the divine qualities more, the world would be the better for it. I believe one play like "'The Passing of the Third Floor Back," in which the mysterious 'Stranger" personifying the qualities of the divine, will ultimately do more good in elevating mankind than a thousand such plays as "The Easiest Way," notwithstanding the force of the latter's terrible picture of the fatal results of weakness and sin.

The tendency is for what we see or read to live in the imagination. We do not stop to think that this is only the result of a play or the reading of a book; the reality of the story, whether portrayed on the stage, described in a book, or suggested in a picture is uppermost.

We are actually living for the time the story of heroism, crime, or whatever else it may be.

What a splendid thing it would be to utilize this tremendous suggestive power in training children by putting in their hands only those books which will stir within them the ambition to become the noblest type of human beings it is possible to be.

It is just as easy to build character with books, with good reading, as it is to tear it down. If the dime-novel type of story makes criminals by its criminal suggestions, the uplifting, inspiring, encouraging books will have just the opposite effect. Many a boy has committed crime while hypnotized by the vivid description or suggestion of crime in a bad book. Many a man and woman has been spurred to a noble, unselfish act while under the influence of some inspiring life story.

The suggestiveness of vice, of impurity in some of our literature is responsible for many blasted hopes and blighted lives. The downfall of many a ruined life began in the dry rot of a perverted imagination. Few of us ever realize how, by a subtle form of mental manufacture, repeated acts of the imagination weave themselves into a mighty tapestry, every figure and fancy of which will stand out in living colors in the character-web of our lives, to approve or condemn us. The greatest power given us, to bless or ban, is the imagination, which, without self-control, would ruin a saint.

As he thinketh in his heart, so is he.— Proverbs.

8

MOTHERS AND DAUGHTERS

As pure as a pearl. And as perfect,—a noble and innocent girl. — Jean Ingelow.

A DAY laborer in St. Paul's Road, London, recently found a six-hundred-and-fifty-thou-sand-dollar pearl necklace which had been lost, though supposedly stolen. After the workman had turned the necklace over to the police he found one of the pearls which had become detached in his pocket. Being entirely ignorant of its value, he tried to trade it in several public houses for a glass of beer, but the barmaids, equally ignorant, thinking it an ordinary bead or marble, would not take it. This pearl which the man could not exchange for a glass of beer proved to be worth twenty-five thousand dollars.

How many young women have ignorantly bartered their priceless pearls of virtue for a bauble, traded it for a few luxuries, pretty clothes, jewelry, or an evening's entertainment or excitement, without really knowing what they were doing, with little more knowledge of the real value of the pearl of great price which the} had exchanged for a bauble than this poor London laborer had of the value of the pearl he tried to exchange for a drink! How many beautiful girls who seek questionable associates and who think they are seeing life and getting away from what they regard as puritanical home rule, away from hated chaperonage, realize the preciousness of that which they may be thoughtlessly flinging away for a little excitement, a little false pleasure! They do not understand that a single indiscretion may ruin their whole future. Their mothers have never explained to them the terrible risks they run of losing that which, once lost, no wealth or position can ever restore. They have never told them that no fortune, however large, can compensate for the loss of their pearl of great price.

If girls, when they begin to go out from the home, were properly armed and safeguarded with a scientific knowledge of themselves; if they were informed of the marvelous precious-ness of the jewel of virtue, which holds sacred the power entrusted to them by their Creator for the purpose of the miracle of reproduction, the wonder of motherhood, it would be an almost unheard of thing that any girl should sell herself cheaply, or thoughtlessly. If girls were reared with the idea that life itself is cheap in comparison with their virtue, not one normal girl in a million would part with that precious gift for any price.

The average girl has been brought up in the belief that there are certain questions, certain things in her life, about which she is not supposed to know anything. No matter how much she may be troubled or perplexed by those things, by the vague yearnings of her nature, by emotions which she cannot understand, yet even her mother is not sufficiently close to her to talk about these matters or to give her any instruction or information whatever regarding them. Social conventions, traditions centuries old, have hitherto commanded silence upon the most important facts of life.

Yet, as a matter of fact, the best possible insurance of a girl's virtue and the protection of her character, is in knowing the whole truth about her body. Such knowledge, far from detracting from a girl's innocence strengthens it to remain firm against vicious assaults.

I know a mother in Washington, the wife of a man of national reputation, who had a most charming daughter, a girl of superb physical and mental endowment. Her great beauty and intellectual brilliancy attracted many admirers. The mother, like so many mothers of past generations, did not realize the dangers that confront young girls who are reared in utter ignorance of their sex nature, and never talked with her daughter on this vital question. She herself had been reared with the idea that it is a subject which girls should never think of, much less discuss. She was an easy and indulgent mother, too, and her daughter, as she approached womanhood, became spoiled by the attentions of men who had flattered her beauty and brilliancy. Self-willed and headstrong, she drifted absolutely beyond her mother's control. Finally the girl went on the stage, where she was especially exposed to temptations.

Being utterly ignorant of her sex nature and the dangers and pitfalls that surrounded her, the girl very soon fell a victim to unprincipled men, who hunted her as hounds hunt deer. She got in with a fast set of people, learned to smoke cigarettes and drink cocktails, and in a short time formed other vicious habits. Though a brilliant actress, she ultimately lost her grip upon her popularity on the stage and deteriorated so frightfully that she passed away in an inebriate and drug asylum, a victim of the cruel conspiracy of silence upon the sex question. If her mother had given her proper instruction regarding her sex nature, and had early taught her self-restraint, this wonderful girl, with her magnificent possibilities, might have been saved from a life of disgrace. As it was, she was wrecked in the very bloom of young womanhood; breaking her mother's heart and nearly ruining her father's career. I have often heard mothers say that they did not want their daughters to know that any such thing as immorality existed, that they wanted to bring them up pure and innocent. It is true there is something indescribably beautiful in the innocence, the sprightliness, the ingenuousness, the playful spontaneity of perfectly pure, untainted girlhood. But, my good mother friend, have you ever thought that, while you are trying to shield your daughter from knowledge of herself and the evil of the world, she may be getting information from the most vicious sources, distorted, exaggerated pictures that may lead to her ruin? Isn't it better that this knowledge, which she must sooner or later have, should come from you, who can give her the truth, rather than from illegitimate sources which garble and distort facts in a way that t411 inflame and debauch her imagination? Why not tell her the plain, scientific truth about herself and about her future, what part she is to play in the perpetuation of the race ? It is not scientific facts which demoralize the mind; it is distorted, obscene suggestions that arouse curiosity and inflame passions. The facts will not hurt your daughter, but will protect her against a thousand evils.

Owing to the great ignorance of our girls regarding their own natures and the peculiar meaning of their sex they are easily led astray, when proper training and knowledge in regard to these subjects would defend and shield them. More girls go wrong from ignorance of themselves and of the terrible results of sexual sin than from almost anything else, and parents are responsible for this colossal ignorance. Instead of our little girls living the simple life, which is the only normal life, allowing their natures to develop naturally, they live, at least in our cities, a complex, stimulative life, the very nature of which tends to make them prematurely old. Even before they reach their teens, too, they are teased about their "beaux"; —this at an age when the slightest lightly-spoken sex suggestion should be tabooed. Everything which tends to over-stimulate sexual instinct should be kept away from them, especially during the most dangerous earlier years, when the seeds of ruin are sown in the great majority of girls who go wrong.

Mothers should have frequent heart-to-heart talks with their daughters during their perilous years of adolescence, when rapid changes are taking place in their nature. This is the romantic age when the emotions are awakening, and young people, perplexed by the new sensations, are tempted to do all sorts of foolish things. It is the stage at which mothers should be most watchful of their daughters.

They should tell them how multitudes of girls have been humiliated all their lives, or absolutely ruined, by giving way to foolish impulses when romance was busy weaving her enticing pictures in the imagination.

It is during this impressionable period that young people are most strongly tempted and have an almost uncontrollable desire to see what forbidden things are like. When they get away from the restraints of home they want to see and know hidden things for themselves, to get unusual experiences, to feel the thrill of new sensations. They crave excitement. Their pent-up energies and emotions often so unbalance their minds that they innocently and ignorantly do things which nothing would tempt them to do if they really understood or appreciated their gravity. During this perilous, romantic period the sexual instinct develops more rapidly than the judgment, so that the mind of the growing girl is not always normal. She has not the same perspective as older people, and hence is much more easily influenced and led astray.

Only a short time ago I read of a girl who went to a dance hall with a friend "just to see what it was like." She met one whom she afterwards described as "an awfully nice man," who was very kind, who treated her to ice cream, and asked if he might call on her. The result was that she did meet him again, and, before long, believing herself to be in love, she gave up her position and eloped with the ""nice young man" who proved to be a white slaver. This was the end of the girl who had never known wrong until she went with a girl friend to a dance hall for a few minutes, "just to see what it was like."

Every girl should be so thoroughly posted upon the mystery of sex and what sex relations mean as to realize that a single slip, a single indiscretion at this period may cost her that which is more precious than her own life. It is ignorance rather than inclination that ruins most girls who go astray. They instinctively want to do right. They love cleanliness and purity much more than men do, but the vicious take advantage of their ignorance and play upon their finer sensibilities, their greater sympathy and their longings for love and admiration. How many young girls are mined just because of their innocence and ignorance which really constitute their greatest attraction for the libertine!

During those most beautiful years in girlhood, when childhood is receding and womanhood advancing, when the maiden,— standing with reluctant feet Where the brook and river meet,— peers with a mixture of longing and shrinking into the mysterious, unknown future, she needs most of all the care of a wise, loving mother. During those years the romantic faculties and the imagination are especially active, and, not having yet developed the judgment and wisdom which come from experience, girls at this period, if not properly instructed, are in great danger of doing all sorts of silly things. They have a great love of adventure; all of their instincts are clamorous and insistent, especially the sexual instinct which imperiously demands explanation. The result of these far-reaching physiological changes is often the development of qualities which the mothers cannot understand. These are the years in which girls should be very close to their mothers; when they need the guidance of wisdom and level heads, without the bad results of constant suppression and over-chaperonage. In other words, at this time girls need liberty, not license, tempered, restrained, and safeguarded by wise love, for it is during this romantic phase of it that their life is set, that the trend of character which largely decides the girl's future is determined.

It is fatally easy during this transition period to slide into the meshes of entanglements which mar the character and which often cripple, if not ruin, the whole life. This is the time when many girls are unconsciously led into entanglements with men of whom they know practically nothing, which compromise their reputation and seriously injure them, even when they are perfectly innocent of any wrong, but have only been indiscreet.

How many mothers have been brokenhearted over the sexual wrecking of daughters who might have been saved by proper instruction! How many daughters commit suicide every year because of the sin against which their mothers never even cautioned them during their adolescence or before the age of puberty I

How little mothers who have been silent on the sex question realize that perhaps a few heart-to-heart talks with their daughters, enlightening them upon the subject, would prevent them from making shipwreck of their lives!

Only the exceptional girl could ever be induced to commit a sin against her own body if she were properly instructed, if she realized that she was bartering the very jewel of her soul for a mess of pottage.

It is estimated that only five per cent, of those who go wrong know what they are doing. The ninety-five are girls who never heard of such a fact as sex relations.

You mothers must know, if you stop to think, that the great majority of girls do not talk much about their chance male acquaintances. Even now your own daughter, whom you think so innocent, may have met some man of whom you know nothing, and whose acquaintance may prove dangerous to her. You cannot be always with her, and every time she goes out on the street she is liable to meet men who have no compunction at leading young girls astray. Only the other day I heard of a man of wealth and good social standing who offered a girl of seventeen the protection of his umbrella in a rain storm, and from that led her on to. her ruin.

Men of this sort play upon a girl's vanity and her instinctive love of pretty things, fine clothes, and tasteful surroundings, to win her confidence and affection. Then there is a promise of marriage, and then,—well, the story is an old one, and we all know how it ends.

The majority of girls who go wrong in this way are easy-going and pleasure-loving. They have not been brought up to develop force of resistance; they have not been taught the protecting power of a vigorous "No." An untrained, weak nature is a fatally poor equipment for fighting the battle of life and the insidious, hypnotizing enemies of virtue. A trained will and the power of self-mastery would save thousands of girls from untold suffering and ruin.

A love of finery, a passion for clothes, is assuredly no excuse for an easy hold on virtue. Neither does it excuse those mothers who have never taught their daughters that their unsullied purity is the very basis of all that is noble and worthwhile in life, who have never cautioned them against the evil that may be wrought by their love of pretty things, their desire to live in ease and luxury which they have not earned.

One of the most difficult things in the world for a mother is to see anything wrong in her own child. She is blind to its faults, and often, after the worm of impurity has already eaten its way into her girl's heart and is blighting her life, the mother does not see it.

I have never known a mother whose daughter went wrong who did not say that she never doubted her child was all right, never dreamed that harm would come to her. There are many things that girls do not tell their mothers, and it is a strange thing that this is especially true in matters of the sexes, their flirtations, their loves, their romantic experiences. In multitudes of cases their mother is the last person they would ever think of making their confidant, possibly for fear of repression, or increased chaperonage, the cutting off of their liberties, or because few girls are ever close enough to their mothers to talk over such things with them.

Few girls ever reveal their unfortunate experiences with men, even to their mothers. The very nature of the sexual relation tends to secrecy, even with one's best friend. This is notably true when a girl is conscious of having done wrong or been guilty of the least indiscretion. It is all the more imperative, then, that a mother should be so close to her daughters that they will keep nothing from her, that they will reveal their inmost secrets to her.

It is often difficult for a mother to tell what is going on in her daughter's heart, no matter how devoted each may be to the other. But every mother ought to be able to tell something about it from her own experience. She must know how hard, probably impossible, it was for her to tell her mother about some of her love affairs. No girl whispers her love secrets into her mother's ears simply because she is her mother, unless she has been trained from childhood to make a confidant of her.

Every mother, however, no matter how ignorant or how badly trained herself, has had experiences and knows many things, knowledge of which would be of untold advantage to her daughter. Why does she hesitate to tell her? Why hide from her knowledge that may shield her from great evil before marriage, and probably from great suffering even after marriage?

A well-known woman writer, discussing this subject, says that one would think that many mothers go on the principle that falling in love and getting married are merely accidents, like being struck by lightning, which is so unlikely to happen to their own daughters that it isn't worthwhile to prepare for it.

It is too true that the average mother treats her daughter as if she never expected her to marry; for the girl comes clear up to the altar practically in utter ignorance of what is before her, without one single valuable lesson from her mother about herself and what marriage means. She has simply followed a blind instinct which has bidden her to mate. She thinks of married life as a continuation of her courtship, a blissful experience with a congenial, worshipping companion. She is utterly unprepared for the rude shattering of her maiden dreams which so often follows marriage for the romantic, uninstructed girl.

It is criminal to allow a girl to go through the nuptial ceremony without any idea of the real significance of the step she is taking. She should be as thoroughly prepared for marriage and all that awaits her afterwards as she would be prepared for her entrance to college or for a professional career. There is no other step a human being ever takes so important as marriage, yet there is no other for which less preparation is made. How many mothers bitterly blame themselves afterwards for the untold suffering such lack of preparation brings to their daughters. They know very well that they might have prevented the wreckage of innocent young lives. They are powerless to repair the evil results of their false modesty, their prudish ideas of preserving what they called the sweet, beautiful innocence of their daughters.

9

PERILOUS *PLEASURES*

Man is first startled by sin; then it becomes pleasing, then easy, then delightful, then frequent, then habitual, then confirmed.— Jeremy Taylor.

There is no vice so simple but assumes Some mark of virtue on his outward parts. — Shakespeare.

In Kipling's fable of "Barrenness," the slave of vice is asked to surrender, one after another, his trust in man, his faith in woman, and the hopes and conscience of his childhood. In exchange for all these, the demon leaves him a crust of dry bread!

When a man seeks questionable pleasure, he should always try to think of what he must pay for it, of his condition after he shall have eaten the forbidden fruit, of what he will have lost, and of what will have gone out of him, for he will never be quite the same again.

If we could project ourselves into "the moment after," how many follies we should not commit! If we had enough imagination, we would do our repenting before instead of after the evil deed.

There is no other human experience so disappointing to the great promise it makes as experience in vicious pleasure. There is a fascination in regard to it, a morbid curiosity about it which often lures one on in quest of the forbidden, the unlawful, to "see what it is like," but the quest invariably ends in bitter disappointment. There is a fleeting exhilaration in the draining of the cup of false pleasure, but there are bitter dregs at the bottom; the poison of the serpent, which afterward stings and torments the victim, is concealed in every wrong act, however alluring in its promise.

No one has ever been able to explain the philosophy of the fascination of evil, the call of the wrong, the lure of sin. It is an opiate to those who are susceptible. They are fascinated by the evil, when they know it injures them, much as a bird is fascinated and drawn to it by a snake, even though it knows the reptile is its deadly enemy.

This pull of sin, this lure of wrongdoing seems to deaden the sensibilities, to paralyze the will. Its effect on those who yield to it is similar to that of opium on victims of the drug habit. They know perfectly well that it is their enemy, that it demoralizes their faculties, deteriorates their brain power, saps their vitality, and will kill all that is finest and noblest in them, and yet the fascination of it pulls them on.

Right here in its hypnotic, mesmeric pull comes the danger of wrongdoing. It is in its power to soothe the moral sense, to deaden the conscience that it gets its strongest hold on its victims. It acts like an anesthetic, an opiate to the moral sensibilities, so that the wrong at the time does not seem so very wrong; and the wrongdoer does not really grasp the full meaning of his act, or appreciate the vicious influences of the evil spell that holds, that enchains him.

We all know something of the terrible suffering of those who are habitually lured by evil, when they have come out from under its mesmeric spell. The shock of returning to their senses after they have recovered from the effect of the vicious anesthetic sometimes unbalances the mind. They endure agonies from the humiliating consciousness of wounded self-respect ; they despise themselves for wallowing in moral filth. The reaction is sometimes so great, so terrible, that people commit suicide.

I have seen a habitual drunkard, after a week's debauch, during which he plunged into all sorts of excesses, come out of his sinful orgy a total wreck. The awful lure of drink drew him to take into his mouth the enemy which he knew would steal away his brain, his good sense, his judgment, his self-respect, and would leave him an easy prey to every other form of evil. Yet the temptation to sin, once yielded to, pulled the victim irrevocably into its toils.

Some people, when tempted to do bad things, think they can silence the still small voice within by resorting to drink or drugs. They imagine that by drowning the accusing voice they can better enjoy the debauch, but they pay the price afterwards. There is no escaping the penalty of wrongdoing. Many a man despises himself, perhaps for years, for some violation of virtue, or some wicked debauch indulged in when his better nature was lulled into quiescence by some deadening anesthetic of temptation.

- Thus one of the most subtle and dangerous /things about sin is its inherent, fatal tendency to soothe, its soporific influence, which paralyzes the will power and leaves the victim helpless. There is a sort of lure, or glamour, about certain forms of wrongdoing, which hypnotize a man so that he is not quite himself. He cannot act with his usual force of choice. There is a subtle mesmeric influence at work in his brain which dazes him and gives him a sense of intoxication, and he is for the moment the victim of one of the strongest impulses, that of his animal nature.

Perverted sexual instinct above all others, affects the judgment and makes the victims blind to their own welfare. Sexual sinners, under the spell of their infatuation, cannot see the awful, the degrading consequences of their wrongdoing. On awakening, however, the sense of the guilt which comes from the consciousness of sexual taint hangs over the mind like a pall.

No one ever indulges in sensuality who does not despise himself afterward when the God image reasserts itself and shames the wrongdoer. I have heard a young man say, after a sensual debauch, that the tortures he suffered were a thousand times greater than the momentary pleasure gained by the gratification of his animal instincts.

No happiness worth the name is possible when procured by the violation of any sacred law of our nature. There can be no real or lasting pleasure in an evil deed, because it shocks the divinity within us which always applauds the right and condemns the wrong. This is perfectly natural, because, being God's children, we have inherited His qualities. His instinctive hatred of all sin. It is the God nature m us that suffers every time we do wrong; it is the sense of outraging the God image in us, our ideal of manhood or womanhood, that puts a sting in the vice that we thought would be pleasure. This sense of outraging our own conscience, this insult to the divine within us, turns the fleeting pleasure into lasting pain.

One has only to look at the sad, unhappy, sin-stained faces of the women of the street, to listen to their hollow, mocking laughter more pitiful than tears, to get a powerful object lesson in the disappointment, the awful disillusion of vice. There is no possibility of extracting happiness from it. All there is in it is a little temporary excitement, a nervous exhilaration, the foam at the top of the glass which hides the deadly poison at the bottom.

Hypnotize ourselves as we may, we cannot hide the truth that enduring happiness can only come from doing right. The moment there is self-accusation, self-condemnation, a wounded self-respect, the fancied pleasure is gone, the after pain has more than neutralized it. The rebuke of the conscience for the wrongdoing infinitely more than balances any little measure of false pleasure that comes while the brain is intoxicated, the senses hypnotized by passion. People who violate the laws of their higher nature sooner or later pay an awful price for it.

A noted burglar tells what a fearful fascination there is in planning how to enter a house and to get away all the valuables he can secure without being shot. The very daring of it, he says, seems to draw a curtain over the crime and to blind him to its terrible consequences.

If it were not for this misleading, deceptive lure of all forms of vice, it would lose its fascination. If vice only carried with its alluring picture the opposite picture of its fatal destroying power, there would be no such thing as vice.

The tempters, the purveyors of evil, the seducers of youth try to increase the lure of sin. They use all their arts to make it attractive.

The new devil of the twentieth century is not like the old. He has lost his horns, has exchanged his traditional satanic dress for up-to-date modern attire. He has put off his repulsive appearance and become fascinating and attractive. He is exceedingly magnetic. He does not frighten or drive away his customers by his appearance; he allures, he draws them by every seduction he can command. He has adopted the latest psychological business methods. He does not attempt to force his victims. He merely suggests, insinuates, lures. He keeps his hoofs out of sight. His tail is covered by a dress coat.

The Bible tells us that the devil cast out of the swine said his name was "Legion." This is certainly the name of the modern devil. His name and his forms are legion. He hides under innumerable subtle temptations. The pitfalls he digs for his victims are often covered with flowers. Ruin and death are cunningly hidden under the guise of pleasure.

The wrong road is made very alluring to a youth. He hears entrancing music which dazes his senses; the god of pleasure puts him, as it were, under a magic spell, and he stands bewildered, intoxicated by the allurements which beckon him. The broad, joyous road to death looks- far more attractive, far more fascinating than the straight and narrow path of wisdom; and, if he has not been properly trained, if he has not been warned of the pitfalls in the way, if he has not learned how to control his passions, he is likely to take the wrong road.

Most of the glittering temptations which beset youth and older people, too, come after dark. It is a strange fact that whatever is wrong, whatever is demoralizing, cannot bear the light. Sunlight is an enemy of vice. Darkness, seclusion, mystery,—these are its accompaniments. Comparatively little of the sinning of the world takes place in the sunlight.

Somehow, when God's sunlight shines full in the face of a man, it makes him ashamed of violating the sacredness of his nature, of defiling the divine within him.

Our idea of a personal devil is that he is always working in the dark, that the light is poison to him, that he cannot carry on his Satanic operations in the sunshine. The counterfeiter, the burglar, the murderer, the seducer, the man who leads innocence astray, and all his other emissaries do their base work in the dark, out of sight. Crime lurks in the byways, the alleys, the dark places, the unobserved entrances. It shrinks from the open gaze of day. The blessed sunlight is an enemy of weakness, an enemy of sin.

If a fraction of the frightful expense caused by crime in every large city were expended in lighting up all the dark, dismal places, especially the slums, making the streets, the alleyways and byways as nearly like the daylight as possible, it would diminish crime immensely and would prove a tremendous investment for the city.

When men are about to do wrong they want to get out of the light into the dark street, away from the public gaze, away from the observation of their fellowmen. When a man goes to indulge his criminal passions, he wants to get away from observation. He would be very low who would dare openly, and before those who know him, whose good opinion he craves, go into the haunts of vice. If men were obliged to come out into the open, into the light, with their nefarious deeds, if they were obliged to do them before the eyes of their fellowmen, they would never do them, they could not be induced to.

If we could throw wide the doors which hide vice in a great city; if we could open the windows and let in the sunshine; if we could draw aside the curtains from the opium dens and all the other resorts of sin; if we could turn on the light, take away the mystery, the secrecy which surrounds it, vice would largely disappear from the face of the earth.

Before men who make claims to respectability go into these vicious places, they look up and down the street to see if by any possibility there is anyone in sight who knows them; then they sneak in and sneak out again, ashamed, disgusted with themselves, their self-respect wounded. They hate themselves for their debauchery, despise themselves because they have been something less than men, because they have allowed the brute in them to silence that still, small voice of manhood, which always calls for the manly thing. I have known groups of college boys to go to a city at night and indulge in drunken, vulgar debauches, and then loathe themselves for it months afterwards.

Beware of the pleasure that looks different in the morning, that makes you despise yourself when the daylight comes; the pleasure which has a reaction, which makes you feel that there is something sacred gone out of you after you have tasted it, which makes you think a little less of yourself, even if you do not actually hate yourself for it.

Yes, darkness seemingly tends to bring out the evil in human beings. The brute side, the Edward Hyde side of Dr. Jekyll in every character, is a night prowler. When he sleeps at all it is in the daytime like the owl and some of the wild beasts; he doesn't like the light. Most of his damage is done in the nighttime.

The majority of people who go wrong are ruined after dinner or supper, when they are through with their day's work. This is the time when the Satan in us, the propensity to evil, the temptation to do all sorts of forbidden things, is especially strong and active, and our power of resistance correspondingly less.

One reason for this is that during the daytime most of us are busy with our work, which is our best friend. It is our great protector, which shields us from a multitude of temptations that appeal to the unoccupied mind, to people out of work, or to those who are habitually idle. A man or woman who is kept busy in making a living, in useful work has fewer temptations to do wrong than the one who is merely seeking amusement. The human mind was made for action; and, when it is not usefully employed, like a piece of unused machinery, it deteriorates very rapidly. In a very literal sense, one's task, be it even drudgery, is his life preserver.

Young unmarried men are peculiarly exposed to danger at night. A married man loves his home, and so has less temptation to wander about after his day's work is done.

His family is his balance wheel, the great steadier of his character. But the young unmarried man, having no home ties and no responsibilities, unless he is thoroughly trained in self-mastery and loves his books and is always improving himself, often succumbs to the flaring and dangerous amusements, the many alluring temptations of the night, especially in our large centres of population.

The whole influence of our modern city life is calculated to over-stimulate the lower nature; and, unfortunately, the city offers all sorts of opportunities for secret indulgences in vice. This makes cities much more dangerous for the young than the country and the smaller towns. No one knows and no one cares what a lone boy or girl in a great city does, and the worst feature of the dangerous fascinations of all the city's lures from vile sources is that their appeal is strongest, their power to tempt greatest just at the time when young people are struggling with an inner passion, which utterly bewilders and surprises them, especially if they have had no safeguard of knowledge thrown up to protect them.

It is the first step that counts, whether on the up or on the down grade. Job tells us that "man is born to evil as the sparks fly upward," and it certainly seems to be the great trouble with many of us that we are more inclined to take the downward than the upward step; that, instead of obeying the call of the higher man and ascending to the heights where purity and blessedness dwell, we are but too ready to listen to the call of the beast and go down to the depths. And oh, it is so fatally easy to yield to the wrong after the first false step! After the first sin it becomes easier and easier to do wrong, until the habit is formed and the protest within becomes fainter and fainter, less and less insistent, until gradually self-respect dies out and the downward course is accelerated.

Thousands of women have regretted all their lives the drinking of their first cocktail, or allowing the first kiss, the first embrace, or other familiarity of their male companions. Tens of thousands of men have taken their first step to ruin and utter degradation by yielding to the temptation of their first convivial glass with "the boys," or to that of entering some den of vice "just to see what it was like."

When men are doubtful of the true state of things, their wishes lead them to believe in what is most agreeable. — Arrianus.

What! know ye not the gains of crime
Are dust and dross; Its ventures on the waves of time
Foredoomed to loss?—J. G. Whittier.

10
FATHERS AND SONS

Knowledge is power.
Diogenes struck the father when the son swore. — Robert Bubtok.

It is a wise father that knows his own child. — Shakespeare.

"I HAVE noticed," said the late William Acton, M.R.C.S., "that all patients who have confessed to me that they have practiced vice lamented that they were not, when children, made aware of its consequences; and I have been pressed over and over again to urge on parents, guardians, schoolmasters, and others interested in the education of youth, the necessity of giving their charges some warning, some intimation of their danger. To parents and guardians I offer my earnest advice that they should, by hearty sympathy and frank explanation, aid their charges in maintaining pure lives."

Ignorance is the cause of much of the criminal perversion of the noblest of human instincts. We have been emphasizing in educational matters the fact that "knowledge is power." Now We are beginning to find that knowledge, pure, sane and scientific knowledge in sex matters, is a youth's greatest protection against evil. Many human wrecks have been ruined through ignorance.

What would you think of a father who would build a ship for his son, teach him every detail about its construction, and equip it completely, but who would fail to put a compass on board to tell his son anything about navigation, and would then start him out across an unknown ocean? What would be the chances of the boy's reaching port in safety? Yet many a father thus sets his son adrift, without moral compass or rudder, upon the high seas of life! He sends him into the midst of temptations and dangers, without a word of advice or guidance in regard to the perils that may assail him from within and without, without teaching him anything of the meaning, the use, or the abuse of a passion which he feels developing within him, but of whose mysterious nature he is totally ignorant!

It is a strange thing that men who have nearly been wrecked on the sex rocks themselves, knowing the frightful risks and the perils in the path of youth, do not warn their sons. Every father knows the ordeal his boy will have to pass through during the early years of his life, and his silence in regard to it is cruel, criminal.

There is no other way in which you can render your son such valuable service as to instill into his heart the idea of the terrible havoc which uncontrolled, abused, or misused sexual instinct will bring to him. To be forearmed, protected by scientific knowledge of the dangers of uncontrolled sexual instincts, is as necessary for a youth as to be provided with a chart showing the position of the rocks and reefs, the dangerous eddies and currents in his course is for a navigator. It is a terrible thing to allow your son to run the danger of being morally wrecked, to take such risks, not only with his health, happiness, and success, but also with the health, happiness, and success of those who come after him, just because you do not like to speak of such a delicate matter or do not quite know how to do it. He will think that you are ashamed to speak to him about a function which the Creator did not think it beneath him to create in such a marvelous manner. He will probably think that you yourself have done something to be ashamed of, and that you cannot bear to speak of the matter to him.

The majority of fathers seem to think that everything connected with the moral and spiritual training of their boys is none of their business, but that all that must be attended to by the mothers. But there is a period in youth when the father is better fitted even than the mother to instruct his boy in sex matters. He knows even better than she does the temptations to which a growing youth will be exposed from within and without. He can warn him against pitfalls of which she, perhaps, may be ignorant. He can better understand the nature and development of his unfolding passions.

There is no other period in the life of a youth so beautiful, so interesting, so sacred, as the critical period approaching puberty.

During these short years his whole character is usually determined,— his physical vigor, his manner, his voice, his mental powers.

Sexual abuse or forbidden indulgences during this stage so sap the vitality as to dwarf and blight both physical and mental development. A perverted imagination at this age has a frightful effect upon the entire nature. The symptoms of such a condition can often be noticed in the gradual change in the youth's manner and disposition. He avoids the society of others. He keeps by himself. He blushes and stammers in the presence of strangers. He shrinks from his former close communion with his mother or even his father. He does not enjoy being questioned about himself. He does not like to face people or look them in the eye.

In the average boy the sexual instinct is probably at its height from fifteen to seventeen years of age, and the sexual desires are then most insistent. This is the time of gravest peril in his career; and, if proper information on the subject is given before the desires are fully developed or indulged in, the boy will be in an infinitely safer position than if left in ignorance because he will know what it all means, and will be better prepared to meet temptation.

If you can guard your son against the misuse of the sexual instinct and keep him from self-defilement up to seventeen years of age; if you have fortified his mind with healthy information upon the subject, he will be comparatively safe thereafter.

Now, it is a splendid thing when your boy is approaching puberty to ask him frequently if anything is troubling, or puzzling him; if he has any problem with which you can help him.

Every boy is going to have a confidant, someone to whom he can tell his secrets, to whom he can whisper his hopes and ambitions which he would not breathe to others. We take it for granted that his mother will stand nearer to him than any other person; but every boy will have some male friend who will stand in a peculiar relation to him, one which even his mother cannot fill. This friend, this confidant, should be his father.

The discovery has recently been made that the marvelous modification of a boy's physique and mind before puberty is due to the action of the sex fluid which normally, is absorbed into the blood and other secretions, where it performs its miracle of transformation into masculinity and virility, but which if abused, wasted or lost, causes a corresponding loss in the youth, makes him so much less a man and so much more a woman.

How easy it would be for a father to show his boy that his sexual organs were set aside for a divine purpose and that any abuse of them will mar his whole life and possibly ruin his career, to say nothing of the tremendous suffering and danger which come from the horrible diseases that often follow abuse of the sexual instinct.

If you begin early enough, it is comparatively easy for you to gain your boy's confidence, so that he will instinctively come to you with anything that troubles or perplexes him in regard to sexual matters. From infancy, he should grow up to feel that no one can take your place; that you stand in a peculiar relation to him, which no one else can fill.

A boy's temperament and disposition have a great bearing upon his sexual development' and excitability. A very emotional and precocious boy, even though he be quiet and sedate and his parents may think that his mind has never been tainted, may be suffering untold agonies from habits which he has formed, probably, because he knew nothing whatever of their baneful effects.

Many a boy suffering thus has longed to have his father ask him a straight question about himself, because this would give him an opportunity to open his heart on the subject. Young men have told me that when boys they often took long walks with their father and took pains to be with him at every opportunity, longing, hoping against hope, that he would broach the matter which was troubling them,— but never a word came on that subject.

No matter how innocent a boy may be, if he has reached the age of puberty, it is infinitely safer for you, his father, to ask him to tell you honestly and plainly all about himself, than to keep silent on questions which so closely affect his health and happiness, his whole future well-being. Perhaps many times he has attempted to approach the subject himself and the words have stuck in his throat. He has thought, "If my father with all his years and wisdom does not mention this matter to me, it must be a terrible thing for me to speak of it to him. There is something mysterious about it. It must be one of the things which he regards as unmentionable, something to be ashamed of." Many boys reason thus and think that their father would reprimand them severely for even having these forbidden thoughts in their mind.

I have known boys whose hearts were almost breaking for clean, pure, accurate information in regard to the mysterious force which they have felt growing within them, and which they have been unable to understand, but never a word of explanation has come from their parents. Is it strange that boys should hesitate to speak to either fathers or mothers on a subject which they, with all their experience and wisdom, for some mysterious reason treat as if it did not exist ?

Do not think, then, because your boy never says anything about these tabooed questions, that he is not in danger of contamination or that he is not already being contaminated. Youths, naturally, will not talk about these things without encouragement, and if you have not brought up your son to look upon you as his chum, as his best friend, one to whom he can open his heart of hearts, he is in danger. One impure companion may contaminate his whole life before you realize it. It is a crime on your part to keep anything back from your boy which he ought to know; and you know a great many things which would be of wonderful help to him. You know, too, that whole schools, colleges, institutions of all kinds, are often honeycombed with the misuse or abuse of the sexual instinct, and that, in innumerable cases, wrong, morbid information upon this sacred subject has been the beginning of ruin.

The church fathers used to teach that the sexual desire is evil, is of the devil; but we now know that the impulse itself, rightly directed, rightly controlled, is the very insignia of manhood, the very force which vitalizes and gives virility, spontaneity and power to the personality.

Teach your boy that the quintessence of his vitality is dependent upon the maintainence of his sexual integrity, that any impairment or abuse of the generative functions upon which the reproduction of the race depends, which are so intimately connected with every cell of the body, involves a loss of physical and mental creative energy which neither physicians nor drugs nor any advertised remedies can restore. Impress upon him the fact that his health, his future success and welfare will all depend upon his preserving physical and mental vigor, and that the most dangerous leak in those matters is caused by abuse of the sexual instinct. Show him that the proper use and the proper restraint of this instinct is the very foundation of life and character.

Tell your son that a large percentage of those who have lost their grip upon themselves are sexual wrecks in one way or another; that many of the men who are headed for the poor-house, headed for failure, the amount-to-nothings, the nobodies, the mere human shadows, the burned-out beings one sees on every hand are those who have been to a greater or less extent emasculated through sexual indulgence. Their vitality and stamina have been sapped; their self-respect killed, their efficiency destroyed, through lack of self-restraint, perhaps on the very threshold of manhood.

Caution your boy that incontinence, especially before complete growth, or in any unlawful way, results in both physical and mental dwarfage. Oftentimes indications of this are shown in a high squeaky voice, scant beard, thin hair, small flabby muscles, morbid sensitiveness, and moroseness. These are some of the signs of lost manhood through the unnatural drainage of the life force. The unfortunates who exhibit those signs are forceless, characterless, weak, inefficient. In short, there is no other early loss which works such havoc in the whole life, physically, mentally, and morally, as sexual wastage and abuse.

There is nothing else so insidious, so fatal in its blasting, blighting influence as the entrance and entertainment of the first impure thought, the performance of the first impure act. Notice how quickly deteriorating and destructive forces begin to operate on a person who violates the laws of chastity and purity. In a few months, even the purest girl may become lower than the animals. It seems as if the Creator regards the integrity of this instinct, upon which the very life, character, and destiny of the race depend, as so sacred, and has placed such a terrible curse upon its degradation that there is no human evil so great as that which follows its violation or abuse. The man who becomes dishonest, or even commits crime, doesn't become so thoroughly demoralized, animalized, brutalized, doesn't stoop so low as he who violates his sexual integrity. The most frightful diseases known to mankind are never generated in right living, never developed among people who live purely and cleanly; but the moment human beings transgress the sacred law of chastity they pay an awful penalty, the price of body, character, and soul destruction.

The best physicians tell us that there is nothing else which will so completely deplete and devitalize, so quickly sap that strength and vitality which could otherwise be turned into power and efficiency, as the abuse of the sacred sex instinct. Sacred, I say, because by means of it the Creator has made man his partner in the perpetuation of the race. Sacred, I repeat emphatically, because all that is beautiful and clean, all that is grandest and noblest in life, all that is worthwhile, depends upon its integrity.

Fathers should give their boys specific reasons for the necessity of living chastely, purely.

They should show them that they cannot from any point of view afford to be devitalized. Most boys are ambitious to make physical records, and if a father will show his son that not only will his spiritual nature be ruined, but that nothing else will so fatally sap his vital energy and physical force as by tampering with his sexual instincts; that the force which wins in athletic contests, as in life's battle, will be seriously impaired, and that he who indulges in secret sins is liable to become a physical and mental nobody, unsexed, he will make a lasting impression on his boy's mind.

Teach your son that it is only during the years when the sexual function is intact, during the years of its integrity, that men achieve anything worthwhile; show him that men who have sapped their sexual life by excesses and abuses have become partially unsexed, and with the unsexing have lost their mental vigor, their creative energy, that force which is back of courage, back of initiative, back of all power and efficiency. Point out to him that to the degree in which a man becomes emasculated does he lose his forceful qualities and tend to become a nobody. Show him how the great failure army is full of these devitalized, emasculated beings who have lost that vitality which must back up all achievement, that creative force which is the secret of all effectiveness, resourcefulness, and ingenuity. Make him understand that executive power evaporates with the exhaustion of sexual vitality.

Stamp it indelibly on your boy's consciousness that all his future, his success, his reputation, his happiness, will depend upon the preservation of his physical vigor. Teach him that the greatest things that will come to him in this world are husbandhood and fatherhood, and that his future wife's happiness and well-being, his children's destiny,—what life will mean to them, their achievement, their happiness, their welfare, the character of their own descendants, —are in no small degree in his hands, and that all these immeasurably important things depend mainly upon the vigilance with which he guards the purity of his own sexual life.

In other words, show him that just in proportion as he preserves his sexual integrity and purity will he tend to become a complete, full-rounded, vigorous, masterful man.

Some fathers seem to think that merely warning their sons to keep away from vicious companions will protect them from the foul sources of contamination. But mere "don'ts," negative formulas, will never safeguard a youth. The only way to protect him is by giving him positive instruction which will raise his ideals, increase his self-respect, and make him think more of himself.

Without giving specific reasons such as I have outlined, to which many more might be added, a father might preach to his boy until doomsday about the thing being wrong, and even wicked, and yet not make any positive or lasting impression. But when he gives him reasons for continence which appeal to him, he makes a salutary and permanent impression. This is where the father's influence especially comes in, because no mother or teacher, however affectionate or faithful, can put herself in a position to really appreciate a boy's situation. The father alone can fully enter into it. He alone can completely realize and sympathize with his son's feelings during his dangerous years.

A boy who is properly instructed in sex hygiene will resent every insult to a woman, no matter whose daughter or sister she may be; for he will have been taught to reverence woman, and because of her comparative physical weakness to consider himself her natural protector. He will regard any injury to a woman, no matter what her class or condition, as a crime against womanhood, and also against his own manhood. He will never forget that one who contributes to a girl's ruin, directly or indirectly, is guilty of a crime, and that this crime totally unfits him for marriage; that it mars his ideal of womanhood, and that he can never have quite the same regard for women, can never quite have the same respect for them or for himself as before.

The father worthy of his fatherhood should instill into his boy's mind such a high ideal of womanhood, such a profound respect for her person, that any suggestion of impurity or indelicacy regarding her sex nature would be unthinkable. He should teach his boy how wonderfully sacred the mother instinct is, how pure and clean; and how imperative it is for his own future happiness, for the welfare of the home and the race, to protect females from insult, from abuse, or from any unholy liberty.

Every boy should be trained with the idea that he is the protector of woman. He should be as ready to protect any other woman from insult as he would his own sister.

In other words, I believe that it is possible to train a boy to have such lofty ideas of chivalry and the sacredness of the female sex that unholy desires and foul passions will never master him. Every time he is tempted to do wrong, the image of his ideal of the girl he hopes some time to make his wife, will stand out before him and so shame him that yielding to wrong will be unthinkable.

Nothing else which you can possibly do for your boy will mean so much to his future as to instill into the very marrow of his being the resolve to come to his wedding day with his ideal of womanhood as pure and unstained as the driven snow; to preserve his own purity as the most sacred thing in his life, and to come to the altar as clean in mind and body as the girl he is about to marry. If you train him so that, whenever he is tempted to violate the sanctity of the sex instinct, he will bring up in his mind's eye the image of his ideal of womanhood, it will be a wonderful help in the practice of self-control. It will kill temptation and make him ashamed of the mere thought or suggestion of wrong-doing.

Some sins are unforgivable, and sexual sin is one of them. The destruction of another's character, pushing a human being down towards degradation, for the sake of a temporary sinful gratification, is a crime against one's own soul, and a properly instructed youth will understand that there is no real pleasure that there can be none, in the commission of such a crime.

If any of you fathers find that your son has been so unfortunate as to contract the habit of self-abuse, remember that he is in a perilous condition, and do not frighten him by unnecessary harshness. He is already suffering all he can endure. I have known fathers by their cruelty at such times to blot out all hope in their boy's mind that he could ever get relief from his trouble. Yet hope and expectation of relief are absolutely imperative, and often the only things that will save a youth in such peril. His mind is already depressed. He is melancholy and morose. This is the time when he needs your sympathy, not your criticism, not your condemnation. Do not condemn him with your head; take him to your heart; advise him; get his confidence; show him that you can help him. Above all else, keep him out of the hands of quacks!

There is no other subject which so troubles and worries the average youth of a certain age as the fear that something is the matter with his sexual life. The very secrecy which surrounds it tremendously aggravates his worry, because he does not dare consult his parents about it. Not one boy in a thousand, under such circumstances, would frankly go to "his father for advice, for he feels guilty; and he would not dare to go to an older friend, or even to the family physician. There are medical quacks who know this only too well, and they take every possible advantage of his delicate situation.

There are thousands of parents who think that their boys have never known evil, that they cannot by any possibility be contaminated, and yet they may be constantly answering advertisements concerning "lost vitality," "lost manhood," and the "errors of youth." These parents little realize the tremendous harvest which the quacks are reaping from their sons, through the effects of their subtle advertisements and criminal literature describing the results of lost manhood.

Away with this foolish criminal mask of silence which leaves your son at the mercy of such charlatans! If you have not safeguarded him with proper instruction at the outset, at the most dangerous period in his life when he has stood tiptoe on the threshold of opening manhood, at the very door of his future, at least come to his rescue now and save him from becoming a victim of all sorts of quacks, who will bleed him, mislead him, and possibly drive him to utter ruin.

Faith in womankind Beats with his blood, and trust in all things high Comes easy to him; and, though he trip and fall, He shall not blind his soul with clay.

— Alfred Tennyson.

11
SOWING WILD OATS AND THE HARVEST

The virtues of the man and the woman are the same. — Antisthenes.

I am ignorant of any one quality that is admirable in woman which is not equally so in man! I do not except even modesty and gentleness of nature; nor do I know one vice or folly which Is not equally detestable in both.— Dean Swift.

"Who are responsible for the introduction of venereal diseases into marriage and the consequent wreckage of the lives of innocent wives and children?"

Answering his own interrogation in the preceding paragraph, Dr. Prince Morrow says, "As a rule, men who have presented a fair exterior of regular and correct living,—often the men of good business and social position,—the men who, indulging in what they regard as the harmless dissipation of sowing wild oats,' have contracted syphilis."

There is no crime followed by more vicious

consequences than that which has been designated by the apparently innocent phrase, "sowing wild oats," nor is there any other which has hitherto been treated so indulgently by society or been so lightly regarded for the most part even by men and women of blameless lives. In fact, people have seemed to consider it really necessary for young men to get this experience and to believe that they would be stronger and wiser for it afterwards. We might as well say that a piece of marble is whiter and purer because there is an ink stain on it. The Agricultural Department at Washington might as well advise farmers to sow weeds or thistles with their wheat in order to get better crops.

Yet many youths have been given the impression by their own fathers, or by physicians, or have gathered from something they have read, that for health reasons they should gratify the sexual desire in the best way they can until they are married.

How often we hear intelligent, educated fathers indulgently say of immoral sons, "Boys will be boys, and they will be all the stronger for sowing their wild oats."

The idea that a youth would be better fitted

for life, would be stronger, wiser, more normal, for the experience of sowing his wild oats— that is, for indulging in immorality, in vulgarity,—is one of the most pernicious and fatal delusions that ever crept into the human brain. The father who thinks his boy must have his wild-oats-sowing season in order to become a man is not fit to bring up a child, and the State should take it away from him.

Yet there are fathers who encourage their boys in the practice of immorality. I know of a noted physician who wrote his son in Yale advising him, for the sake of his health, to find some girl in New Haven with whom he could practically live while going through his academic course! A father who would give such counsel to his son should be indicted by a grand jury for soul murder. The result in this instance was that the son went to the dogs, and finally loathed his father for the criminal advice that ruined his health and his career at the outset.

Many another young man, while sowing his wild oats, has formed vicious habits which have dogged his steps and handicapped him all his life. If a man of coarse fiber, he has probably sunk to the level of his own bestiality and has failed to realize the true value of his "might have been,"— of the higher, better, more successful and happier life which he has lost. But to a naturally fine-grained man, under such conditions, life often seems but a mockery, with its chalice of joy presented invitingly to his lips only to be dashed rudely away and shivered to fragments by the demon of passion who accompanies him everywhere. He may put on a brave front to the world and to others seem even happy, but to himself his forced laughter echoes mockingly and drearily through the empty chambers of his soul. Such a man might well exclaim with the gifted "poet of remorse,"—

Though wit may flash from fluent lips, and mirth distract the breast,
Through midnit hours that yield no more their former hope of rest;
'Tis but as ivy leaves around the ruined turret wreathe,
All green and wildly fresh without, but worn and gray beneath.

A great many boys are brought up with the idea that it is not very sinful to visit disorderly houses—that it is not a millionth part as bad as the seduction of a pure, innocent girl. I have heard fathers say that they would rather their sons would consort with fast women, that they would rather that they should seduce innocent girls, than marry socially beneath them. One man I know told his son that the great thing to be careful about was not to get caught in his escapades with women!

Is it any wonder that such infamous moral standards and such base teachings as these not only ruin multitudes of boys, but also imperil the happiness and lives of a multitude of unfortunate girls and women?

To what end is all this? The monstrous fallacy that Nature has so erred in her construction of man that he should become lower in the scale of life than the beasts in order to conserve health is exploded. The idea that incontinence is a health preserver for young men has been set at rest for all time by many of the most eminent physicians in the world. Sir W. R. Gowers, M. D., F.R.S., lecturer of the Medical Society of London, says, "The opinions which on grounds falsely called physiological' suggest or permit unchastity are terribly prevalent among young men, but they are absolutely false. I assert that no man ever yet was in the slightest degree or way the worse for continence or the better for incontinence."

Sir Andrew Clarke emphatically declares, "Continence elevates the whole nature, increases energy, and sharpens insight."

Another distinguished physician says, "It is a frequent observation instilled into the young at all ages: "I am told it is very bad for me to be continent; my health will suffer from it.' No greater lie was ever invented. It is simply a base invention to cover sin, and has no foundation in fact."

In the Year Book of the National Society for the Scientific Study of Education in England we find this significant paragraph: "We expect of physicians explicit and positive contradiction of the fallacy current among men and sometimes sanctioned by medical authorities that sexual continence is very harmful to health."

Authoritative statements might be multiplied not only to bury the ancient lie that un-chastity makes a man healthy, but also to prove that its effect is exactly the opposite.

To put it on the very lowest grounds, I am certain that, if young men knew and realized the fearful risks to health alone that they run by indulging in these gross impurities and dissipations known as sowing wild oats, they would put them by with a shudder of disgust and aversion.

When physicians tell young men who have contracted a terrible venereal disease that, even with constant treatment, there is no possibility of cure in less than three or four years, and that they may never be cured, the sufferers often give way to utter despair. This is especially true of young men who are about to marry. Many of them lack the moral stamina, the courage to make a clean breast of their troubles, or to release their fiancée, to postpone their marriage, and the results are terrible suffering, degradation, and often death from the transmission of this frightful plague.

Not long ago a young man in an agony of remorse and shame put an end to his life on his wedding day. His physician had told him that, owing to sexual trouble, he was in no condition to marry, and that he must postpone his marriage. But the wedding day was fixed, and, too much ashamed to tell the truth to the girl who loved and trusted him, he committed suicide while the terrified bride-to-be waited at the altar.

Another tragic case is told by a prominent physician who was invited to the marriage of a beautiful young girl whom he knew. The marriage was to be a fashionable one, and society leaders where both the young people lived were to attend. A week before the wedding, however, the young man had been "out with the fellows" sowing wild oats, celebrating his last days of bachelorhood. Afterwards he had to consult a physician, who did not tell him that he must postpone his marriage, but said that marriage for him at any time would be a crime. The night before the wedding the young man shot himself.

So lightly has this crime of sowing wild oats been treated, and so ignorant have women been kept of the awful enormity of the consequences, that it is not unusual to hear a romantic girl, who mistakes wickedness for manliness, say, in speaking of a man, "Oh, he is too good. I like a fellow who has sown his wild oats, who has had some experience, who has seen life. I have no use for the man "who knows nothing of the world, who has been brought up in a cage, tied to his mother's apron strings.' "

How little do such romantic girls, how little do any girls or women, realize what they do when they marry impure, immoral men. How ignorant they are of the true meaning of sowing wild oats,—how little they dream what frightful harvests are bound to follow the sowing.

Indeed, in the long run, they are the greatest sufferers, for one of the most terrible results of the sowing of wild oats is the hideous aftermath of suffering inflicted on innocent, unsuspecting women and their yet unborn children.

A distinguished physician estimated that a large percentage of all the operations performed by specialists in diseases of women in this country are the result of venereal infection, and that an equal percentage of all the deaths due to inflammatory diseases peculiar to women are the result of this infection.

In multitudes of cases trusting young wives have suffered untold tortures from vile diseases communicated to them by their husbands who had contracted them while sowing wild oats in their youth. Formerly the helpless victims were kept in ignorance of the real facts by male physicians who would not reveal to them the cause of their suffering and the disfigurement of their unfortunate children.

It is well known that mental deficiency in children, and every kind of physical deformity, even the birth of monstrosities, are a part of the harvest reaped from the wild oats sowing.

In twenty-seven months over six hundred children, the victims of a loathsome disease inherited from their fathers, passed through the most piteous children's ward in a Chicago hospital. All but twenty-nine of these children were under ten years of age, "and," said Jane Addams, "doubtless a number of them had been victims of that wretched tradition that a man afflicted with this incurable disease might cure himself at the expense of innocence." It is a well-known fact that thousands of children who are born blind or become blind at birth suffer this ghastly affliction because of their fathers' sins.

How can a man face an innocent child who bears in its body the evidences of his unlawful passions, who must carry through life the curse of his sin, without loathing himself? A large part of the insane and criminal class, the sexual perverts, the idiots, the imbeciles, the physically defective, and tens of thousands of invalids are such because of this sin of sins.

Everywhere we see wretched, innocent children whose lives will be crippled or totally wrecked because of their father's sin. Many of them are dwarfed, deformed, and have physical or mental defects, or idiosyncrasies which will follow them through life. Verily, the sins of the fathers are visited upon the children, and the children's children.

Think, too, of the unhappy mother, who must often endure the double agony of suffering herself—often undergoing surgical mutilation,—and seeing her children suffer!

Miss Addams cites a pathetic case of a widowed mother in Chicago afflicted with a terrible disease which she had contracted from her husband. The unfortunate mother was so terrified for fear of spreading the infection to her children that she offered to leave them forever if there was no other way to save them from the horrible suffering she herself was enduring.

The number of young women whose health has been wrecked by marrying immoral men will never be known. "How dismal," says Dr. Valentine, "is the history of many a young woman who marries with all the accompaniments of a wedding celebration. From their husbands' latent disease many of them contract conditions which alter their lives and even their characters. They suffer from backache, urinary disorders, localized peritonitis, loss of their healthful beauty, lassitude, hysteria, sterility, miscarriages, or death."

Referring more fully to the awful danger the wife runs of being infected by an immoral husband, Christabel Pankhurst, in "Plain Facts About a Great Evil," quotes Dr. Prince Morrow, who says: "'The conditions created by the marriage relation render the wife a helpless and unresisting victim. The matrimonial bond is a chain which binds and fetters the woman completely, making her the passive recipient of the germs of any sexual disease her husband may harbor. On her wedding night she may, and often does, receive unsuspectingly the poison of a disease which may seriously affect her health and kill her children, or, by extinguishing her capacity for conception, may sweep away all the most cherished hopes and aspirations of married life. She is an innocent in every sense of the word. She is incapable of foreseeing, powerless to prevent this injury. She often pays with her life for her blind confidence in the man who ignorantly or carelessly passes over to her a disease which he has received from a prostitute. The victims are for the most part young and virtuous women,—idolized daughters, the very flower of womankind.' "

It would be hard to name a crime so dastardly as for a man deliberately to defile and poison the body of the clean, sweet girl who loves and marries him; deliberately to inflict upon his children a foul disease,—deformity, idiocy, premature death. Yet this is done, with a frequency which has at length aroused our best physicians to the struggle for public enlightenment and protection.

A prominent physician, invited by the editor of The Ladies' Home Journal to produce statistics on the sex question, says that there are more than eight million people in the United States to-day suffering from the direct or indirect infection of sexual diseases: that in New York City alone there are many, many thousand men and women afflicted, to say nothing of little girls of five and ten years of age who are cursed with the germs of some of those loathsome diseases. The great white plague, according to this authority, is a mere incident as compared with the great black plague. "The horrible and distressing operations upon innocent wives," he says, "the increasing sterility of married women, can be explained and avoided. The ruin of many innocent boys and girls who come in contact with the germs scattered round them can be stopped." He further states, "When I add that over eight out of ten young men from fifteen to thirty years of age are suffering from the direct or indirect causes of this sexual sin, that thirty-five per cent, of these cases will bring mother, grandmother, or children to the hospital, to early graves, you will agree that it is absolutely necessary to speak plainly."

Much of this terrible suffering of innocent women and children is due to what is called professional etiquette among physicians. Multitudes of men have hitherto been shielded in their damnable immorality by physicians under the pretext of this shibboleth of professional etiquette. They are bound to report to the Board of Health cases of such comparatively innocent diseases as measles or chicken pox. If-a case of smallpox, cholera, or some other virulent disease were not promptly reported to the health authorities and all necessary precautions taken to prevent the spread of the contagion, there would be a popular outcry. If a person is found infected with leprosy, the whole country is up in arms, and the unfortunate and wholly innocent sufferer is driven from the community, isolated from civilization. But, simply because men, not men and women, make the laws, physicians are not obliged to report cases of moral leprosy, the foulest and most deadly of all diseases.

One of the most horrible features of moral leprosy is the appalling facility with which its physical contagion is conveyed to the innocent.

Not long ago a very suave and attractive young man on leaving a social gathering in Philadelphia kissed the hands of the five young ladies who had been his dancing partners during the evening. In a short time all five developed a hideous venereal disease which has made their marriage practically impossible, and ruined not only their potential motherhood, but, practically, their lives.

In innumerable cases fathers have communicated this disease to their children by kissing and fondling them. It has been passed along through the exchange of lead-pencils, by putting them in the mouth, by the use of towels, and in countless other ways. Yet the moral lepers are allowed to go unchecked on their death dealing way.

The ethics of the medical profession in regard to cloaking the resultant evils of man's immorality are, however, rapidly undergoing a great change, and the physician of the future who protects the reputation of a moral leper, at the expense of his unsuspecting and helpless victims, will be boycotted by all decent people. He will be regarded as accessory before the fact in contributing to the defilement and suffering of innocent beings. The reputable physician of to-morrow is not going to help the tainted to spread the contagion of the vilest of diseases. Even though the man-made laws support him in concealing the truth, he will not remain tongue-tied regarding moral leprosy when he is in duty bound to the public to report cases of measles.

But the average old-time physician is horrified at the very idea of making public a statement in regard to the health of a patient which would injure the patient's reputation. To divulge a professional secret is dishonorable. But there is no hesitation in making public the knowledge of any other crime, however much it may reflect on the reputation of the criminal.

Knowledge of any other crime against society, any other disease than this, which involves secret sin, is not regarded as a professional secret. The doctor who would conceal the truth about a murder or a robbery because the perpetrator happened to be a patient of his would rightly be regarded as an enemy of society. Why should the crime of silence in regard to an offence which destroys the soul as well as the body of the offender himself, and causes untold suffering, perhaps death to others, be countenanced by the law and the medical profession?

It is about time that the curse of secrct immorality should be dragged out of its hiding place and exposed to the light. If every physician was compelled by law—and it is a crime against society that he is not,—to be truthful in these matters, this black plague of sexual immorality, with its evil progeny, would be tremendously circumscribed. If every young man, every husband and father, knew that his secret sin would be made public, that he would be disgraced in the eyes of his family, his community, there would be comparatively few male—or female—prostitutes. If the sex that suffers most from this great social pest had a voice in making the laws that pertain to it, it would quickly be put under a penalty equal to its enormity. If there was no other reason for giving the vote to women, this one would be sufficient. Men will never legislate against their own sexual sins. There will always be immunity for the sexual criminal until woman gets the power locked up in the ballot.

Already women physicians and women's organizations have succeeded in two states, Iowa and Vermont, in securing the passage of a law which requires a physician to report a case of venereal disease to the Board of Health as he does a ease of smallpox, diphtheria, scarlet fever or measles. It is to be hoped that all the other states in the Union will quickly follow the example set by Iowa and Vermont.

One of the most unfortunate things about the sowing of wild oats is that the practice, when once started,—whose only excuse, let it not be forgotten, is celibacy,—is continued by a large majority of men after marriage and continued not infrequently all through their married life.

It is a strange fact that even many men who lead exemplary lives at home, and who are careful not to do anything which can bring pain to their families, throw off their restraint when they are away from home, in distant cities, and especially when traveling abroad, and do all sorts of immoral things which nothing could induce them to do in their own little village or small town.

A painful instance of this was brought to light not long ago in a large Eastern city, when a man regarded as a pillar of the church and of society in his own town was discovered to be habitually leading a "double life" when away from home. Cases of this kind are all too frequent among so-called reputable men.

The fear of public opinion keeps many men of indifferent virtue straight in small towns. They have a terror of gossip and are afraid of possible social scandal. Pride of their standing in the community, and especially of their position in the church, is a constant restraining influence. The wrong done to wife and children sits lightly on their conscience, but they are held in check by fear of what their neighbors will say. The majority of men would be polygamous but for the restraining influence of their egotism and the fear of the Mrs. Grundy of their small community, but when they go into strange cities they feel a sense of freedom, and, under cover of secrecy and the practical certainty that no one at home will ever know what they have done, they give license to their grosser nature.

This is well known to purveyors of vice, and many of the questionable things which are shown sightseers in large cities are maintained largely for the sightseers themselves. The city people do not patronize them much.

Many indecent places in the city of Paris are kept up mainly for tourists, and are patronized, largely, by men who are quite decent in their home towns.

Men from the country and from out-of-town places who visit houses of prostitution in the cities little realize how much they contribute to the awful degradation of women. But remember, my friends, who loosen up your morals when you go away from home, that every poor girl you find in any of those vile places is somebody's daughter, may be somebody's sister, as dear to some father or mother as your daughter is to you or your wife, that her life is just as sacred in the eyes of her Maker as the lives of your own sisters and mother. Do not forget that most prostitutes were innocent victims lured to brothels to gratify men's base passions.

Do not think, because you are away from home, that you are away from responsibility, that you can get away from the inexorable laws of nature and virtue. If you break them anywhere in the universe, you must pay the price of a stain upon your manhood, the loss of self-respect, the acquirement of personal degradation from which you can never escape. You have contributed to the downfall of human beings. You have contributed to the havoc of their deplorable lives, to their wretchedness, their demoralization. You are personally responsible. You are an accomplice in their ruin, you are in league with their murderers.

Do not hypnotize yourself with the idea that, when away from home, you can drop your moral standards, draw a curtain over your ideals, drag those whom you are bound by every law of your being to protect down to lower depths, and then return to your innocent and trusting families thinking that these wretched girls mean nothing to you because they happen to be strangers. No; you cannot escape the consequences of your sin. It may come back to mock you in the ruin of your own innocent daughter or sister in some resort of vice. In some way or other it will again and again meet you face to face.

Theosophists believe that the man who wrongs a woman, who debauches the souls of others, is in the life beyond the grave perpetually tormented by the spirits of those whom he had injured on earth, that they never cease following him until his soul is purged and purified by frightful suffering.

Whether we agree with this theory or not, we cannot blind ourselves to the truth that there is certainly some place and time for the squaring of all our accounts. We know that the universe is governed by scientific laws; we know that not an infinitesimal particle of matter in this world is ever lost, and that every cause has its legitimate effect. Man cannot escape the working of the universal law. It is just as certain as doom that those men who even contribute to woman's ruin must sometime, somewhere suffer the just punishment of their acts. People who know him in this world may know nothing of his damnable acts, but the soul that sins, no matter how he covers up his crimes, shall ultimately pay their fearful price. In view of all this, the theosophic theory does not seem unreasonable, albeit the sexual sinner does not have to go to the world beyond to reap the consequences of his acts.

Lecky, the historian, speaking of the unfortunate woman, the victim of man's lust, says, "She is the most mournful and the most awful figure in history. She remains while creeds and civilizations rise and fall,—the eternal sacrifice of humanity, blasted for the sins of the people."

How much longer will society sanction this blot on our civilization? How much longer shall we continue to have sex in sin?—to stone the woman and let the man go free, and thus perpetuate the presence of "the most mournful and the most awful figure in history"?

It is "up to" this generation, now that the light of knowledge and truth has been turned on the dark places, to see to it that men's selfish, animal desires shall not continue to blast a large proportion of the very flower of the human race.

The sowing of wild oats, with its frightful harvest of human misery, degradation, crime, and death, must go.

12

MEDICAL QUACKS AND "LOST MANHOOD"

Give me that man That is not passion's slave, and I will wear him In my heart's core, ay, in my heart of hearts. — Shakespeare.

There is a story of a certain man afflicted with a painful disease who had traveled far and wide in search of a cure, and tried all sorts of remedies and physicians without avail. One night he dreamed that a Presence came to him and said, "Brother, hast thou tried all the means of cure?" The man replied, "I have tried all." "Nay," said the Presence, "come with me, and I will show thee a healing bath which has escaped thy notice." The afflicted man followed, and the Presence led him to a clear pool of water, and said, "Plunge thyself in this water and thou shalt surely recover," and thereupon he vanished. The man plunged into the water, and, on coming out, lo! his disease had left him, and at the same moment he saw written above the pool the word "Renounce/'

Now all this time the man had been harboring a secret sin, but in the clear, cleansing waters of the pool he had renounced it,—and was healed.

Renunciation is the price of a strong, clean character, a noble manhood. If you would wear "the white flower of a blameless life," you must renounce the things that lead to sin, you must keep away from the things that would stain your manhood, smirch your honor.

Speaking of his youth, when other young fellows wanted him to be "one of the boys," "to take a drink," Edison said, "I thought I had a better use for my brain. I wanted all the brain power I could get. I wanted to increase the efficiency of my life and not diminish it, not demoralize and benumb it. I did not want to take into my mouth an enemy to steal away my brain. I wanted to do the things which would increase, not diminish my brain power; which would increase, not lessen, my possibilities ; which would increase and not destroy my resources; something which would increase my powers of investigation, of discovery; something which would increase my inventive ability, not destroy it, and I said to myself: "I will let that greatest enemy of the race, that enemy which has taken hold of more men and women, ruined more careers, destroyed more happiness, than anything else in the world, alone.'"

There are several places in the world where clean, pure rivers empty into other rivers which drain large factory districts. The water in the latter is contaminated with all sorts of chemicals and refuse from the factories. It is turgid and dirty. For long distances those rivers sometimes run side by side with quite clean-cut lines of demarcation between the pure and the filthy; but gradually, as they flow down towards the sea, they mingle, and after a while the pure stream is lost. The filthy, muddy stream has absorbed and contaminated every drop of the pure water.

How often we see a similar thing in human life; where the muddy, turgid, filthy stream of impure associations contaminates, arid finally absorbs, the stream of purity and innocence running beside it until both streams merge into one black and murky river.

If you have been so unfortunate as to become soiled by contact with such a foul stream, don't lose heart and think there is no hope of purging yourself of your uncleanness. Above all else, don't go to sexual quacks, or resort to remedies suggested in their advertisements.

Tens of thousands of young men are being seriously injured through the influence of these advertisements, which delineate in the most subtle and suggestive language the terrible consequences of sexual perversion. Frequently their authors slyly distribute little booklets on the street, when there are no policemen about, —for their distribution is against the law,— under the guise of memorandum books, but which really contain poisonous descriptions of the awful results of youthful error and the diseases resulting from sexual sin.

All these medical blackguards are "out for the cash." They have not the slightest regard for the welfare of the young man about whom they seem so solicitous, and they v/ill rob him of his last penny without a shadow of compunction. I have known many instances where they have advised youths to borrow money, or even sell their belongings rather than take the awful consequences that they are assured would follow non-treatment. I have known college boys to pawn clothing, pledge their books, and borrow money of their student friends, ostensibly for other purposes, but in reality to secure the "cure-all" remedy or to get the wonderful "advice" described in these subtle advertisements, which frighten away the peace and happiness of thousands of splendid boys who, perhaps, have made a single false step under great temptation, but who, at heart, are clean and pure.

The quacks tell these victims of youthful error that loss of vitality thus caused is more fatal than many times the same amount of blood drawn directly from the heart,—just as if blood drawn directly from the heart is worse than if drawn from the foot! They describe in lurid colors the symptoms of lost vigor, of lost manhood, and other evils which follow sexual sin. So vividly do they picture these things and so seductively do they work upon the youthful imagination that the victim is constantly watching for and expecting predicted symptoms, until sometimes his mind actually becomes unbalanced. In many cases the perplexed youth is cursed with mind wandering. He cannot focus his attention upon his studies or his work. His parents and teachers cannot imagine what is the matter with him, for they do not see the worm that is eating its way into his heart and slowly blighting the young life long before it comes to maturity.

While the consequences of continued sexual indiscretions can hardly be overrated, there is probably not the least warrant or justification for a hundredth part of the worry and the wretched anxiety of these unhappy youths. Their fears are worked upon by the criminal quack advertisements and the literature of the blackguards who are bleeding them. These vile advertisers become experts in fishing for "suckers." They know how to put out the tempting bait; and, when the victims are finally drawn into a quack's office, he says to himself: "Just as I expected. Those advertisements did the work."

These medical quacks describe the symptoms of the victim of self-abuse in terms something like the following, "Confused mentality in the morning, dizziness on rising, a bad taste in the mouth, a wandering mind, inability to focus the thought and to hold it upon a certain subject. Nervousness, despondency, a feeling of debility, and general lack of energy, ambition, and life." "Solitariness" is also one of the symptoms that they emphasize, an inclination to remain by oneself, to shun people.

Now these are common symptoms of almost every boy and girl during the years of rapid growth, when marvelous changes are taking place in the brain and all the functions of the body. Even the purest, cleanest boys in the world are liable to be affected in the way described when the physical and mental developments in every part of the system are so tremendous.

Of course the quacks do not confine themselves to enumerating such simple and general symptoms of puberty as these. They know very well that there is a close connection between the sexual functions and the brain, so that, whenever there is any trouble with the sexual life, the brain is seriously affected, and this very fact gives them a double hold upon young minds. They know how to picture in their damnable literature the fatal results of youthful abuse and sexual indiscretions and sins. Consequently, those who have any misgivings in regard to themselves fall easy victims to their nefarious appeals.

I have known boys in schools and colleges to be so terrified with fear that they might be sexually ruined that they have not been able to concentrate their minds, have fallen behind in their classes, and in many instances have been obliged to drop their studies and go home. Some youths even become insane, and their parents have thought all along that the whole trouble was due to overwork or ordinary physical ailments.

I wish it were possible to reach every youth in the land to bid them beware of the authors and purveyors of such literature.

They are not in the business for the good of your health, my young friends, but for the good of their own pocketbooks. Their literature is designed to make you think that they are extremely anxious to help you,— that they want to save you from self-destruction. They are well aware how sensitive you are about this subject, and how your fears are aroused, even if there has been in your conduct not the least cause for worry. But they know that, if you have the remotest suspicion that anything is wrong with you, you will be an easy victim to their insinuating appeals. They know very well that, by hook or by crook, you are going to get the money to consult them and to buy their quack remedies. No reputable physician would for a moment endorse these remedies; he knows that there is absolutely no curative virtue in them. These vile advertisers have no secret, no knowledge, no drug, no remedy of the smallest value to give to young men in exchange for their money.

In their advertisements we often see the photograph of an elderly man with a long beard and a benign face, who is described as the guardian angel who presides over an institution founded to save boys "who have made mistakes." As a matter of fact, the actual man who presides over the institution has no venerable beard whatever, but has a blackguard's face, a face so repulsive for its animalism and greed that to publish it in his advertisement would be to drive away patrons. I knew one of the meanest, crudest, most grasping and conscienceless men in Chicago who went by the name of old Dr. Blank, who was supposed to be one of these sages who save multitudes of youths from destruction. Such men as he and their institutions are the vilest frauds. Quacks of this kind should be prohibited by law from practicing their nefarious trade, and their advertisements should be banished from public prints.

If you have been so unfortunate, either through ignorance or otherwise, as to violate the sexual instinct, the first thing to do in order to retrieve your error is to get your mind normal, to get rid of the idea that you are in a hopeless condition, that you are going to the dogs, that you will inevitably become emasculated physically, mentally, and morally. Above all other things, never resort to any advertised drugs or remedies, never read any quack advertisements or literature. They will only poison your mind, and their authors will rob you of every cent you have.

Why, only a little while ago I knew of a poor boy who spent nearly all the money he had for a marvelous electric belt which was going to restore his "lost manhood" and cure him of all evil tendencies. Of course this did him no good whatever. He was simply throwing his money away. He told me that he afterwards spent hundreds of dollars in all sorts of advertised medicines, appliances and devices, and received absolutely no help from any of them. Finally, he met and fell in love with a beautiful, pure girl, and through association with her was restored to his normal condition. He was cured of his obsession, married the girl whose influences had saved his life from wreckage, and is now happy.

Now, my suffering young friend, wherever you may be, remember that, whatever the degree of your sexual sin, you are probably exaggerating your condition. Your mind is not normal, and you are, possibly, so obsessed with the hopelessness of your case that, if at school or college, you may not be able to concentrate your attention upon your studies; or, if at work, whether of a mental or physical character, you may find yourself unable to focus your power and do it intelligently. The most fearful obsessions I have ever known have been developed by splendid youths who have, perhaps in moments of supreme temptation, gone wrong, or who have ignorantly, without any knowledge of the hideousness of their error, fallen into secret practices which have had a fearful effect upon their minds. When they realized the awful seriousness of sexual sin, they completely lost heart, thought there was no hope of recovering themselves, and went down to utter degradation and ruin.

There is no evil so bad that it cannot be ameliorated, and the very fact that there is a strong probability that you are greatly exaggerating the desperateness of your situation should give you confidence to help yourself. Specific suggestions for self-cure treatment are given in the next chapter.

The first thing for you to do, however, is to resolve firmly to conquer yourself, to be a man, and to break away from whatever evil habit holds you down. Keep your mind as sanely and wholesomely occupied as possible, and absolutely free from sexual matters. Read pure, wholesome, inspiring literature that will flood your mind with lofty thoughts and ideals. This will be an antidote to your worst enemies, sensual thought, sensual imaginings, and vicious associations. The purer your thought, the quicker and the more certain your complete recovery.

Do not allow yourself to talk about sexual matters; do not listen to impure stories, or covert allusions to subjects that should be held sacred. Associate only with pure-minded people. Keep much with your sisters and your mother, and, if you have a sweetheart, associate as much as possible with her. The companionship of pure women will be one of your greatest helps in recovering yourself. It will make you ashamed that you ever had even an impure thought.

Remember always that purity is power, creative energy, efficiency, happiness. It must be the very basis of your ideal of marriage and of a home. Remember, also, that you owe it to the girl of your dreams, the girl you hope to marry, to keep your mind, your physical life, just as pure and clean as you expect her to be when you lead her to the altar.

The whole secret of your recovery is not in quack drugs or remedies, but in yourself, your mental attitude, your determination to be true to your best self, to live up to the highest and noblest ideal of manhood which is possible for every normal youth.

When you get a glimpse of the divine within you and experience its uplifting power, when you learn to trust the God in you for assistance, for release from this slavery, you will find yourself and this divinity always in the majority. Nothing, no evil power, can then stand against you. "Chastity enables the soul to breathe a pure air in the foulest places."

On the other hand, there is nothing else which so shuts God out of one's life as gross impurity. The soul of the confirmed sexual pervert ceases to aspire and revels in moral filth. Every act of impurity still further obscures the soul vision.

We forget too easily the sanctity of life. It uplifts a man to feel respect for himself, to feel that life proceeds from God, and that it gathers up in itself all the pain and joy of the past and all the hope of the future. When a man understands this, he willingly forgoes a fleeting gratification in order to keep life pure, strong, invincible.

There is a very close connection between a fine, strong, clean body and a fine, strong, clean character. Very often deterioration of character begins with the neglect of the person and little details of toilet, of the bath, and the grooming of oneself. Absolute cleanliness of body assists greatly in the attainment of mental and moral purity. The consciousness of being clean in every particular adds to one's self-respect and gives an uplift to the whole being, increases ability, clears thought, strengthens ambition, stimulates energy and vitality. A cold bath every morning, winter as well as summer (if you react quickly), is a tonic for both body and mind.

Regular habits, simple fare, plenty of exercise and sleep, and both in the open air if possible, good, wholesome amusements and associating with people of high ideals and noble character,—all of these are wonderful helps in leading a pure, simple life.

But in this, as in every other form of disease or sin, an ounce of prevention is better than a pound of cure. You cannot tell what may come to you in the future, what honor or promotion ; and you cannot afford to take chances upon having anything in your past come up to embarrass or hold you back.

There are many men who have been raised to positions of honor and public trust who would give anything in the world if they could blot out some of the unfortunate experiences of their youth. Things in their early history, which they had forgotten and never expected to hear from again, are raked up when they become candidates for office or positions of trust. These forgotten bits of imagined pleasure loom up as insurmountable bars across their pathway.

I know a very rich young man who thought he was just having a good time in his youth,— sowing his wild oats,—who would give a large part of his vast wealth to-day if he could blot out a few years of his folly.

"Young men, keep your record clean!" exclaimed John B. Gough, his last words uttered on a platform in Philadelphia, at the very instant when death laid its finger on his lips,— words in which the whole life teaching of the eloquent orator are compressed. The young man whose record is clean has nothing to fear. He can have no better help in making a successful life. Even his physical prowess is dependent on his purity record.

The medical directors in our colleges tell us that strict continence is absolutely imperative to the success of athletes who are training for severe contests. It often happens, they say, that, when men have unaccountably failed in such contests, it is afterwards found that they have been violating the laws of chastity and thus have devitalized themselves and so sapped their stamina and grit that they have been easily vanquished by their competitors.

Physicians know that the retention of the sexual fluid makes for mental and physical virility, that it is transmuted into brain power, into creative force and bodily vigor, and that, on the other hand, any drainage of this force results in mental' and moral as well as physical deterioration. Any loss of sexual force, especially before a youth attains his growth, starves and stunts his physical and mental development.

Animal breeders understand this principle. They know that young animals are stunted and never attain their maximum of physical development unless they are carefully guarded from a too early drain and loss of sexual force. Even untutored savages understand Nature's laws and isolate their youths from females until they have attained their complete physical development.

Purity is best protected by a great life purpose. A man with such a purpose is shielded from a great many temptations which come to the aimless. His energy, his surplus vitality, goes out in enthusiastic work.

Constant occupation and pure, high thinking bar the way to impure thoughts and desires. It is in the chambers of an idle life that the spiders of impurity spin their webs. A thousand temptations, which never come to a busy man, tempt the idle brain to all sorts of mischief. The whole family of vice dogs the steps of the idler. Just as vicious characters gravitate toward barrooms and haunts of vice, so bad things, evil things which arouse the passions, gravitate toward an idle brain. As vermin, slime and all other sorts of disgusting things collect in a pool whose water has no outlet, so all uncleanness finds a resting place in a stagnant mind. While the brook was tumbling down the mountain side it was clear and sparkling, but when it reached the valley and stopped working, it became the meeting place for everything that was vile, disgusting, and ugly. The active mind, the man engaged in ennobling work, keeps all his faculties clean, strong, and pure, while the idler, the man who is not occupied in some useful work deteriorates and becomes polluted. Innumerable examples of the disintegrating effects of idleness may be found among the gilded youth who have no other occupation in life than seeking pleasure. If you "hitch your wagon to a star" and keep constantly working toward your ideal, impurity cannot get hold of you. Nothing will tempt you to the misuse or abuse of the most sacred instinct of your being, the sex instinct, the preserving of which in its integrity, in its absolute purity, will alone bring you the greatest happiness and make possible the highest efficiency. Your record will be as clean as that of the Duke of Wellington, of whom Tennyson in his funeral ode, when England was mourning her great hero, said—

Whatever record leap to light. He never shall be shamed.

13

HOW. TO REGAIN YOUR MANHOOD

Virtue is not left to stand alone. He who practices it will have neighbors.— Confucius.

Or, if Virtue feeble were, Heaven itself would stoop to her. — John Milton.

On the 22d of September, 1862, when he had resolved upon the Emancipation Proclamation, President Lincoln entered this solemn vow in his diary: "I have promised my God that I will do it."

That was the first step toward the issuance of that epoch-making proclamation which gave liberty to an enslaved race.

If you are enslaved by vile, impure habits your first step toward freedom is to promise your God and yourself that you will be free. Seal your promise as Lincoln did his by writing it in your diary. Emphasize your decision by constantly repeating it to yourself, or when alone, audibly. The audible self-cure treatment may be used with marvelous results in correcting any unfortunate habit.

In a boys' club in one of our large cities the boys have a self-conducted court in which they affix penalties for the offending members. This is one of the penalties: A boy who has been reported as using profane language is obliged to write two hundred times the sentence, "What a foolish habit this is!" After he has been through this experience a few times he begins to realize that the habit is a pretty foolish one.

If you have smirched your ideals and degraded yourself by vicious habits of self-indulgence, the practice of impurity, whether physically or through a debauched imagination, there is no better way to break these habits, to overcome this practice, than by giving yourself mental and oral, not written, purity treatments, especially before retiring at night. Talk to yourself something after this manner: "I know this vicious habit is destroying my vitality; I am not so vigorous, so virile, as I was before. My brain is not so creative. I am not so robust physically or mentally. I do not think so clearly because my brain has become muddled. I cannot concentrate or control my mind as I once could. I go all to pieces over little annoyances which once did not trouble me.

"This demoralizing habit is placing me at a great disadvantage in life. It is holding me down when I ought to be forging ahead. I know that I have more ability than many of those about me, who are accomplishing a great deal more than I. Now, I am going to conquer this thing which is destroying my vitality, sapping my life, and ruining my prospects. I am going to free myself from it, to recover my self-respect, my manhood, at any cost. I am going to be a MAN, not a THING."

Keep your freedom from the enslaving habit constantly fixed in your mind, and continually strengthen your power to overcome by autosuggestion of hatred of it and the reiterated resolution to fight it to the death.

Flood your mind with thoughts and affirmations which will antidote your sensual desires. Look out for the subtle persuasions of appetite. Repeat again and again your determination not to allow your life to be spoiled by unrestrained passion. Make your denial of its power over you so strong and vigorous that it will help kill your desire. Whenever you are assailed by temptation say:

"It is unmanly to yield to this temptation which is debasing my whole being. No matter if others do tell me that, in order to be a good fellow, to be a sport, to be a 'thoroughbred,' I must do what the other boys do, must know the world, and must sow my wild oats. I know it cannot be right to do that which makes me hate myself. I am certain that the Creator never made that necessary to my health or my growth which makes me despise myself. I cannot afford to indulge in habits which make me ashamed to look myself in the face, which make me blush to meet others.

"I know very well that I radiate what is in my mind, that I shall give the impression of my uncleanness, for whatever is uppermost in our thoughts we are constantly giving out to other minds. If I indulge in this habit others will see the results of it in my face and I shall not be able to look them in the eye. I am only too conscious of having violated the most sacred thing in me, and I shall radiate this consciousness to others."

You must replace the impure imaginings in which you have hitherto indulged by their opposites, by pictures of things that are pure, uplifting, clean, healthy. You must clean up your mind before you can clean up your morals. Mental hygiene is the great remedy, the healing balm for all immoral wounds. If the mind is kept clean the body will follow suit. Pure mind, pure imagination, pure body.

In cautioning youth against that impure visualizing which bewitches and corrupts, Henry Ward Beecher said, "I solemnly warn you against indulging in morbid imagination. In that busy and mischievous faculty begins the evil."

No one can indulge safely thoughts, suggestions or emotions he would not act out in reality without shame or fear. Thousands of the inmates of our penitentiaries began their downward career by imagining criminal procedure; visualizing, innocently perhaps at first, the act of Entering a house at night and burglarizing it. Repeating the criminal thought, the criminal picture, led to the criminal act.

The first sin of the sexual pervert was one of thought, of immoral visualizing, until the immoral thought habit was formed and the acts followed. He must regain his manhood through the same medium—the mind.

As Dr. Quackenbos, the famous hypnotic physician who has had remarkable success in helping sexual perverts to reform, says, it is the continued and unfailing radiation of healthful and uplifting ideas, the holding such ideas constantly in mind, perpetually keeping the mind away from debasing thoughts, these are the potent helps to reform.

Mental hygiene must precede physical hygiene. The mind must be sustained and strengthened by the frequent renewal of your solemn promise henceforth to keep yourself pure. You may vary the words you use, but let your purpose be unchanging, inviolable from the start. Think of the pure good women you know, and say:

"I hereby promise my God to do nothing which will make me think less of myself, which will mar or lower my ideal of womanhood. I despise the thing which keeps me back in life, which tends to make me a failure, or anything less than a man. I will not take the risk of indulging in it a little longer with the hope that something will help me to break the habit later. I know that further indulgence will only bind me more strongly to it, and make my ultimate chances of breaking away from it less and less."

One great trouble with the curing of vicious habits is that many people resolve to quit for a certain time. This is fatal. There is only one way to kill a vicious habit, and that is to strangle it by cutting off the food which nourishes it.

To release ourselves from the power of a long-continued habit, and to form a new one. Professor James said:—"We must take care to wrench ourselves with as strong and decided initiative as possible. We must accumulate all the possible circumstances which shall reinforce the right motive. We must put ourselves assiduously in positions which encourage the new way. We must make engagements incompatible with the old. We must develop our resolution with every aid we know. This will give our new beginnings such a momentum that the temptation to break down will not occur as soon as it might, and every day during which a breakdown is postponed adds to the chances that it will not occur at all. We must, however, never suffer an exception to occur until the new habit is securely rooted in life. Each lapse is like letting fall a ball of string which one is carefully winding up—a single slip undoes more than a great many turns will wind again."

There is no such thing as breaking away gradually from the vice of impurity or any other sin. Dallying with it only gives it a firmer hold on you.

John B. Gough was a brilliant young man. He knew that he had a better use for his brain than to destroy it with alcohol, but he prided himself upon being able to control his appetite at any time. With the arrogance of self-confident youth he said to himself: "John, you are strong enough to stop this drink business whenever you wish to." But before he realized it he found that the tiny wires of habit which could have been severed so easily in the early stages had gradually twisted into a powerful cable which held him in a grip of iron. He found himself a slave where he thought he was master. He knew that if he did not put forth a mighty effort to break the chain that bound him he would never regain his lost manhood. So one night at a temperance meeting, with hand which shook so that he could hardly write his name, he signed the pledge.

Then began a fearful struggle for mastery. For days and nights, without a mouthful of food, and with almost no sleep, he wrestled with the demon which was trying to overpower him. For a whole week he continued to fight that fearful battle with appetite until he conquered. Then weak, faint, almost dying, he crawled into the sunlight, victorious. The man had conquered the demon which had almost slain him.

After this triumph over the forces of evil the possibilities which had failed Mr. Gough in early life began to come back. Little by little he got possession of the great life assets which had slipped away from him while his brain was anesthetized by alcohol. Bit by bit his capital of manhood came back until he had not only re-established himself in the estimation of those who knew him, but became a tremendous power for good.

Once you have put your hand to the plough don't allow yourself to look back, and above all, no matter how hard the battle goes, don't succumb to discouragement. It is not an easy matter to overcome a vile habit, but the power of divinity within you is greater than that of any evil passion or practice, however strong.

When Washington was officially notified of his nomination for the Presidency he was completely overcome, so little did he realize his own greatness, his ability to fill such a high office. He felt that there was no one in the room who was less fitted for such a high position or less worthy of so great an honor. He had little idea of the latent forces and commanding qualities which the next two years would call out of his nature.

Most of us do not half realize our latent strength because we do not exert it. We do not make a loud enough call upon the Great Within of us, our higher, more potent selves.

"Affirm that which you wish, and it will be manifest in your life." Affirm it confidently, with the utmost faith, without any doubt of what you affirm. Force your mind toward your goal; hold it there steadily, persistently, for this is the mental condition that achieves, that conquers all obstacles, overcomes all temptations.

The objective side of man has a wonderful power to inspire and to encourage the subjective side; to arouse the subconscious mentality where all latent power and possibilities lie. Deep within man dwell slumbering powers that would revolutionize his life if aroused and put into action.

The habit of claiming as our own, as a vivid reality, that which we desire, has a tremendous magnetic force in drawing those subconscious powers to our aid. Affirmation is creative. The constant vigorous assertion: "I am purity; I am health; I am vigor; I am power; I am principle; I am truth; I am justice; I am beauty; because made in the image of perfection, of harmony, of truth, of justice, of immortal beauty"—tends to the manifestation of these things in our lives.

Few people realize the tremendous creative power there is in stout self-assertion; in the vigorous affirmation of the divine power of the ego, the "I," the "I am." But those who have once properly put it in practice never again doubt its efficacy.

After he had conquered the alcohol habit and had become the most powerful temperance lecturer in this country, Gough used to describe the struggles of a friend in his effort to break away from smoking, over-indulgence in which had shattered his health. The man threw away all his pipes, everything which had anything to do with tobacco, and said that was the end of the whole business. But it was only the beginning of greater suffering than he had so far endured. His craving for "just one smoke" was so great that he would chew chamomile, gentian, even tooth picks, to deaden the desperate physical gnawing of his desire. In a moment of weakness he bought a plug of tobacco and put it into his pocket, not to chew, but "for company." The temptation was too great and he took the plug out of his pocket determined to stop his agony by one chew. But before putting it into his mouth, some divine impulse stirred within him, and he looked at it for a moment. Then his manhood came to his assistance, and throwing the tobacco from him he cried, "You are a weed, I am a man, I will master you if I die for it!" He did master it by continually asserting his manhood, his power over the thing that was injuring him. "I am a man. I will master you if I die for it."

Audible self-suggestion, which is merely a continuation or extension of the affirmation principle, is one of the greatest aids to self-control. We all know how a resolution is strengthened by the spoken declaration to put it into effect.

There is a force in words spoken aloud which is not stirred by going over the same words mentally. They make a more lasting impression upon the mind—just as words which pass through the eye from the printed page make a greater impression on the brain than we get by thinking the same words; as seeing objects of nature makes a more lasting impression upon the mind than thinking about them. If you repeat to yourself aloud, vigorously, even vehemently, a firm resolve, you are more likely to carry it to reality than if you merely resolve in silence.

There must be no shillyshallying weakness either in your resolutions or affirmations concerning the loathsome vice of impurity. You must be very positive in your affirmation of power to overcome your dangerous habit. If you simply say to yourself, "I know that this thing is bad for me; I know that if I continue its practice, it will interfere with my success and destroy my health and happiness, but I fear I shall never be able to overcome it; I know it will be a fearful struggle, because it has such a terrible grip on me," you will never make any headway.

Always stoutly assert your ability to conquer. Say to yourself, with the utmost conviction, "I was not made to be dominated by such a vice. God's image in me was not intended to wallow in this filth. I can never use my ability to the best advantage if I continue in it. I shall never be the man my Creator intended me to be, that I am capable of being, while I harbor this secret enemy which will sap my force, waste my vitality, and weaken my chances of success in life. It is making structural changes in my body, destroying my ability to think, blurring my moral sensibilities. I am done with it at once and forever. The appetite for it is destroyed. There is something divine within me, the God man, the 3tamp of my Creator, that which makes me perfectly well able to overcome this thing, which is not of God, but of the devil."

The trouble with most people in trying to overcome evil habits or to create good ones is that they do not use half their will power, or, what is even stronger, their power of conviction which can be greatly increased and intensified by constant affirmation. Our resolutions are weak, wishy-washy. We do not put vim enough, grit enough into them. It is only the vigorous resolution that conquers.

When a general burns his bridges behind him, cuts off all chances of retreat, he knows that his men will fight with a desperation which would not otherwise have been possible. As soon as you have seriously committed yourself to your resolution and have burned your bridges behind you, this very committal will call to your aid mighty hidden resources of whose very existence you were ignorant. But as long as you leave open a way of retreat, and think that perhaps when the temptation becomes too strong you will indulge just a little, you will not bring out your greatest resources. These only respond to the desperate call, the wireless "S. O, S." of the soul.

Have nothing to do with the companions that would drag you down. Cut loose from everything that suggests, that tempts you to indulge in impurity. Get out into the country, if you can, into the woods, away from the allurements of vice. Say to yourself, repeatedly and firmly, out loud if you are alone, "I hereby take a sacred oath never to repeat this cursed thing. It is an insult to my ideal of womanhood, an insult to my future wife, a crime to my unborn children. You are a deadly, beastly, degrading, soul-killing, efficiency-paralyzing habit; I am a man. Let's have it out now once for all. Let's have an understanding with each other right here as to who shall dominate this divine human machine— my body. There is no chance for both of us in this establishment. Either you have got to get down off the throne and let me rule, or I shall have to quit and turn everything over to you, which I shall never do.

"Now, you vile Thing, you have disgraced me for the last time. Never again can you humiliate me, make me despise myself. Never again can you drag me into the mud and mire of beastly indulgence, or make me the slave of desire or passion. I am done with you. You have had your last grip upon me.

"There can be only one ruler here; and that one is going to be myself. I don't propose to allow you to ruin my life, to force me to carry in my very face the signs of my weakness, of my degradation and the triumph of vice over me. You have humiliated, disgraced, and insulted me long enough by your damnable domination, making me admit that I am a nobody and that I have lost out in the great race for success and happiness, making me acknowledge that I have not enough strength of mind to stand up against a single, vicious, degrading habit.

"Now, I defy you, and I deny your power over me. Hereafter I am going to walk the earth as a conqueror, not as conquered; as a victor, not as a victim. Hereafter I am not going about like a whipped cur. I am going to face the world with my head up. Hereafter I am going to be master here. You have gotten hold of the wrong man if you think you are going to keep me down any longer.

"Your chief strength over me in the past has come from the law of repetition. Every time I yielded to you made it easier and ever easier to yield again. By this same law of repetition, through the power of affirmation, I will free myself forever from your grip."

You will be surprised at the uplifting sensation, the stimulating thrill, the new sense of victory which will come from your first triumph over your enemy. You may feel weak, exhausted physically in the beginning, but you will grow stronger daily. Those verbal heart to heart talks with yourself will give you new courage, new power to overcome. They will start a new hope center in your life and sustain you in the battle. By the constant repetition of victory over your lower nature you will in time gain complete self-mastery.

Another thing of the utmost importance is to have your mind in good condition when you retire. Prepare your mind for sleep with a mental bath, excluding from it every vicious thought, all unholy visualizing. Be careful what you see at night. Do not go to exciting or questionable amusements, for whatever disturbs your sleep will aggravate your trouble. Put yourself in a worshipful attitude. The mind adapts itself to the body's position. The assuming of an attitude of reverence and devotion toward your Creator, the lifting of the ideals, by dwelling upon pure, clean thoughts before composing yourself to sleep, will be a tremendous help in restoring you to health and purity.

It is a terrible thing to be a slave to any weakness or vice which saps our energies, dwarfs our efforts and lessens or ruins our chances in life. But these things are only as strong, only as real as we ourselves allow them to be. The most degrading habit can be broken link by link as it was forged link by link.

It is holding the thought that you cannot break away from the degrading habit you have contracted that gives it power over you. That power would instantly be broken if you believed, and asserted your belief in your own power to break away from it. But as long as you believe you are a hopeless victim of the habit that enslaves you, you will be. When you begin to affirm that you are free; that you are no longer the slave of vice, you have already written your Emancipation Proclamation.

Vice repeated is like the wandering wind, Blows dust in others' eyes, to spread itself. — Shakespere.

Virtue alone outbuilds the pyramids;
Her monuments shall last, when Egypt's fall.
— Edward Young.

So dear to heaven is saintly chastity
That, when a soul is found sincerely so,
A thousand liveried angels lackey her.
Driving far off each thing of sin and guilt. — John Milton.

Note. —The subject of health in general, including in particular a description of the proper measures to be taken for the recovery of vigorous manhood, is in itself an extensive one—too extensive to be discussed in this volume.

When youthful errors have undermined the physical powers, one is face to face with problems that are often times serious. But we have the assurance of specialists in the field of sex hygiene that once injurious habits are absolutely discontinued, their effects may in every case be overcome by proper physical upbuilding and the attainment of a sane and normal mental attitude.

Those who seek full and complete information on the anatomy of the human body, and also in regard to the hygienic measures—diet, exercise, bathing, etc., best adapted to counteract physical shortcomings of every sort, cannot do better than to obtain from the publishers of the present work the five volumes of "Macfadden's Encyclopedia of Physical Culture."

These volumes present in complete form, for ready reference, information on every aspect of body-building. Attention is directed to the descriptive notice following the conclusion of this book.

14

WHY THE 'UNFORTUNATE WOMAN'

'Tis a "glorious" prowess, forsooth, with a word.

To wound the trusting and tame the proud. E'en as a leaf by a breath is stirred,

A spray by a dewdrop bowed; And so the battle goes bravely on.

And hearts get hardened as tongues flow free. And swells the blazon, "I conquer you.

Lest you should conquer me."

When the rose of thine own being

Shall reveal its central fold. Thou shalt look within and marvel.

Fearing what thine eyes behold: What it shows and what it teaches

Are not things wherewith to part; Thorny rose! that always costeth

Beatings at the heart.— Jean Ingelow.

Nearly half a century ago a boy of nineteen, whose parents were in moderate circumstances, went to a large city at a distance to take an advanced course of study" To eke out the small allowance his father could afford, he did janitor work, put on plastering laths by the thousand, japanned metal castings by piece work, and drifted into canvassing for books under a general agent who trained him and under whose tutelage he soon became very successful, taking up a new book when his territory had been covered for the one in hand in its turn. At length he took up two companion books by Dr. George H. Napheys, "The Transmission of Life," for men, and "The Physical Life of Woman," for women. They were very good books, giving information every one should possess on matters of sex and sexual hygiene; and, as they were of interest, or should be, to all, the agent directed that the ground should be covered without skipping a house, as had been done with other books of interest only to special classes.

In one house the canvasser sold one of the women's books to a young woman who seemed much interested in it and questioned him very earnestly about it before purchasing, and who then asked him to wait a moment until she could call in some friends and draw their attention to the book,—as the young man, contrary to his usual custom, carried a supply of books for immediate delivery with him. She soon returned, accompanied by half a dozen young women friends, each of whom, by her advice, bought a book. They all seemed to be similarly interested, and gave him the names and addresses of friends to whom they wished him to present the merits of the volume. He had not called upon more than one or two of these friends before it suddenly dawned upon him that there was something queer about the whole matter; and, on inquiry, he learned what he had at first not so much as suspected,—he had stumbled into a house of ill fame at first, and had been sent to other houses of the same kind. But what impressed him most was that every inmate, or nearly every one, bought a book, one of the most moral and plain-spoken ever published.

Naturally, because of the sales, he made the rounds of all but the lowest brothels in the city, and sold many books. But what astonished him most—deeply impressed him, in fact,— was that not once, in all this round, was he himself canvassed for immoral purposes. Indeed, although some of the women he met were ignorant and somewhat slangy of speech, not one made a remark or even a suggestion which would be considered improper in any company. The earnestness and bearing of the boy no doubt had something to do with this, but it was almost painfully evident that the women were very seriously, were even sadly interested in the subject matter of the book, and were imbued with a sort of missionary spirit that led them to wish to extend its aid and counsel to as many of their unfortunate class as possible.

The boy, grown to manhood, has been solicited many times in large cities by "women in scarlet," but never with any licentious temptation whatever. Instead, in such instances, he has always pitied the poor creatures, and he has never forgotten the glimpse he got, in canvassing, of traces of their better nature which still survived their fall even in world-condemned and pariahed prostitutes.

He has since married and reared a large family of children. Influenced by what he learned while canvassing, he has had repeated, careful, sympathetic talks with his boys, beginning when each was six years old, and has persuaded his wife to have similar talks with the girls. All the children are leading moral lives, and not even a rumor of anything else has stained the life of any of them.

In answer to a question as to whether the " unfortunate woman" is a victim or a contributor to her own vicious career, John D. Rockefeller, Jr., founder of the Bureau of Social Hygiene in New York City, replied: "I say unhesitatingly that in the vast majority of cases she is a victim. Prostitution, as now conducted in this country and in Europe, is very largely a man's business; the women are merely tools in the hands of the stronger sex. It is a business run for profit, and the profit is large.

"It is my belief that less than twenty-five per cent, of the prostitutes in this city would have fallen if they had had an equally good chance to lead a pure life. That they have been dragged into the mire in such large numbers is due to a variety of circumstances, among which are poverty, low wages, improper home conditions and lack of training, the desire to gratify the natural craving for amusement, pretty things, etc.; but, while all of these and many others may be contributory causes, man is chiefly responsible for their fall."

This statement of Mr. Rockefeller is supported by Lieutenant-Governor Wagner, chairman of the State Factory Investigation Commission of New York. Speaking of a recent report of the Commission, he said:—

"Women lose what is best and most sacred to womanhood because of starvation wages paid in some greater New York industries. Startling conditions have been disclosed. We have found that thousands of women receive less than six dollars a week, and in many instances as low as four and one-half and five dollars a week.

"How do these women live? We know that they cannot live on these low wages. They cannot secure even the barest necessities of life, much less help maintain a family, as some of them have to do.

"Who pays this difference?

"That is the serious problem that confronts us. Many of these women literally starve. In other cases there is a loss of health, a physical and mental breakdown, and the worker becomes a charge upon the people. In still other cases some of these unfortunate women are rendered an easy prey to the basest temptations, particularly in the larger cities."

The detectives of the Juvenile Protective Association in Chicago recently arrested and convicted seventeen men and three women who were plying their miserable trade in the rest room of one of the big stores. They were taking advantage of girls waiting to look over the "Help Wanted" advertisements in the papers, which they could not afford to buy.

The department store furnishes fruitful grounds for the procurers, both male and female; for, while the doors of factories are closed to outsiders, the store doors are always open to everybody.

Dapper young slave traders will go into a store and make little purchases of the pretty girls, often trying to flirt with them, giving them little presents and inviting them out for the evening; and, the first thing these girls know, they are in the procurer's toils. Women who keep dives often invite salesgirls to their homes. These women usually spend large sums for clothing, and they often tell the girls behind the counters, especially the attractive ones, that they could earn much more money in a much easier way than by working so hard in the stores!

Many salesgirls who wait upon rich customers and who see all sorts of pretty things, beautiful dresses and lingerie, which the young girls long to possess, piled up about them everywhere, are constantly placed under fearful temptation. Of course a well-trained girl, of strong, resolute character, is in no danger of succumbing, but when we remember the numbers of naturally weak, ignorant, and wholly untrained girls many of whom live in loveless homes, often with dissolute parents, we can understand their craving for affection and protection, and why they are more easily tempted by the men who make love to them, and who— though of course the girls do not suspect them —are all the time trying to betray them, to work their ruin.

Martial music, color, glittering uniforms have a strong psychological influence even on staid practical people. They stir the blood of the young and work them up to a state of abnormal excitement. Most young girls are peculiarly susceptible to the influence of this martial glamour. There is something about a military uniform and a soldier's life which fascinates them.

Jane Addams says that, during an army encampment near Chicago, a great many girls were so fascinated by the presence of the young soldiers in the city that they completely lost their heads. An investigation showed that some had even climbed out of the windows at night, after their parents were asleep, and gone out with these men. One girl was found by the agent of a protective society hurrying away from the encampment late at night. The tears were running down her face, and she was sobbing as if her heart would break. She was so overwhelmed with her wrong that she was totally unconscious of the presence of the society agent, who heard her say over and over to herself: "O Mother of God, what have I done! What have I done!"

Their natural love of romance, their spirit of adventure, their passion for innocent fun and play, have been taken advantage of to lead many to their ruin. If those traits had been directed into wholesome channels in childhood, most of the unfortunate girls, whom the world condemns, and upon whom society turns its back, could have been saved to lives of usefulness and happiness.

Who can estimate the awful human depravity, the tragedies, that have resulted from young people frequenting cheap theatres, suggestive picture shows, and other low amusement places, with all their demoralizing influences? One of the most dangerous elements in those places is that they cater so much to the animal instincts. In their very advertisements, they appeal to the sexual instinct. In most dance halls, improprieties in the dancing and in the association of the sexes are fostered and encouraged, aided by the exciting influence of drink; the desires are inflamed, and means of gratification are even provided.

The severity and penuriousness of some parents who are constantly prodding them to earn more money, to increase the family income, are responsible for the downfall of their daughters. The family loyalty to which many of these girls have been trained frequently leads them to support a father who drinks and gambles, even though they are often brutally treated if they do not bring home what the parents consider sufficient money.

A well-known sociologist cites a typical example of this kind. A delicate, anemic girl who was a dishwasher in a restaurant found herself unable to earn what her parents expected of her. The long hours of confinement and the heavy work were too much for her weak frame, and the meager contents of her pay envelope were often further reduced by her off-days when ill. Her miserable parents not only upbraided her for not earning more, but often cuffed and slapped her; and her brothers and sisters, who were stronger and earned somewhat more than she did, accused her of laziness and of not doing her part.

The girl became so discouraged that when a waitress in the restaurant in which she worked told her that she could double her money by making noon hour appointments in a near-by disreputable hotel, she decided to try to earn her pay in an "easier way." It was many months after she entered this disreputable house before her parents knew of the change, as she continued to bring her money home regularly every week.

Years after the death of the ignorant mother, who had abused her for her meager earnings, the unfortunate girl referred to her with the hope that "the old lady is now suffering the torments of the lost for making me what I am!"

Of course, girls of this class who have not been properly trained do not fully realize the moral iniquity of their conduct or its awful consequences. They only see the contrast between the tempting picture put before them— the large pay, the beautiful clothes and exciting experiences of the evil life,—and their own poor, meager earnings, shabby clothes, and monotonous existence. The stories of the large amounts of money which others make in their illicit trade are fearfully tempting to weak-minded girls who have such a hard time to make a decent living, to clothe themselves respectably, and in many instances to give a large part of their salary for the support of their families.

It is true that a girl's virtue should be dearer to her than life itself, and that the very thought of selling it for material things—for anything whatever,—should fill her with horror; but, in any consideration of this question, we must not forget the ignorance, the lack of training, the environment and home conditions in such cases as those of the little dishwasher, and the constant temptations and evil allurements with which those unfortunate girls who are led astray are usually surrounded.

The flourishing condition of commercialized vice is very largely a result of poverty, of discouragement, of desperation. Tens of thousands of business men in this country, even in comfortable circumstances, are perpetually haunted by the fear that they may not be able to support their families and that they will be disgraced by failure. How many men become discouraged when they are out of work for a time and commit suicide to put an end to their troubles!

What shall we say, then, of the multitudes of girls who can barely earn enough to keep them alive, even in their healthiest, most attractive years? What shall we say of the temptations that beset them on every hand? Is it any wonder that the spectre of poverty demoralizes the minds of some of them and that they become easy victims of the tempter?

Is it any. wonder that the inexperienced girl who perhaps does not know where her next meal is coming from should fall an easy prey to some man who is a professional expert in undermining a girl's virtue, expert in vicious diplomacy, in suggestion, in hypnotism, expert in taking advantage of the very virtue of the girl, her longings for a home of her own, her yearning for the food of starved affections, her longing for somebody to love her?

Just imagine the temptation of a man who is struggling against a great passion for drink, trying his best to live a temperate life when his indomitable appetite is clamoring for satisfaction! Imagine this man's plight when his companions pull him into a barroom where everybody is drinking, hilarious and exuberant, and where he is insistently urged to join the rest,—what would be the probabilities of his resisting?

The poor girl who is solicited by the white slave procurer is equally tempted. He appeals to her longing for a home, her yearning for love. Perhaps her life has been barren of social opportunities, barren of friendship, barren of love, and this tempter holds out all sorts of inducements to her. He pretends to love her; he tells her he wants to marry her, that she is the girl of all girls he has ever met who understands him. She is bombarded with all sorts of suggestions and temptations. Is it any wonder that in a moment of weakness, and perhaps when she is weary, she accepts a drink to brace her up, not realizing that this will relax her moral sensibilities, and that she has already unlocked the door which her betrayer will never again let her lock?

Poverty and desperation and betrayal largely explain why so many delinquent girls and deserted women enter the underworld. Many a girl has explained her yielding to temptation and an evil life by saying that in a moment of utter weariness and discouragement she "went out with a man."

They are not the most robust kind, it is true, but it is well known that "morals fluctuate with trade." In hard times, when business is poor, during the dull season, and especially in periods of great commercial depression, the evil resorts have a great influx of recruits.

In investigations conducted by the various girls' protective associations, many instances have been found where girls had gone hungry for months, because they could not earn enough to pay their room rent, their laundry bills, and the price of their meals, before they succumbed to temptation. They had given in only after suffering untold tortures, through fear of starvation, and because their pride kept them from appealing to charity.

Many girls are led into earning money in questionable ways because of their pride, a pitiably false pride to be sure. They cannot keep up appearances; they cannot pay for their room or board; their landlady presses them, and then there are the appealing letters from home for help,—all these things, which the great world outside knows nothing of, are at work to undermine self-control and break down courage.

One girl pressed in this way explained to those who were trying to rescue her that she "had sold out for a pair of shoes"! This unfortunate finally yielded to the temptation to earn money in an illicit way after she had been trying in vain for seven months to save money to buy a pair of shoes. She paid three dollars a week for board, sixty cents for carfare, and had only forty cents a week left for all other expenses out of her four-dollar salary! It was impossible to buy the shoes.

The fearful struggle for a livelihood, the false standards of living in this country, and the terrible strain to keep up appearances are responsible for the downfall of tens of thousands of unfortunate girls, who, in their distressing poverty, see the evidences of wealth and luxurious living flaunted in their faces wherever they go. When we add to this the damnable wiles of the procurers, who are always on the lookout for girls who are discouraged and distressed, it is not strange that so many of them are dragged into the underworld.

The effects of over-strain, over-fatigue, and insufficient nourishment tend to undermine the moral sensibilities. Think of a girl trying to make a living by inserting eyelets in shoes at the rate of two cents for a case of twenty-four pairs! Is it any wonder that the powers of physical and moral resistance become weakened by this perpetual over-strain, over-speeding, which is common in every industrial line?

Is it not easy to see how young immigrant girls, who are ignorant of our language, our usages, our streets, our social customs, often become easy victims of evil men who take advantage of the great difficulty they have in getting work in our overcrowded industrial centres, and who impose on their innocent credulousness with all sorts of stories?

Innumerable causes have been in operation to assist the white slavers in their nefarious work. Among other things a troubled, unhappy mind and mental discord tend to demoralize self-control and lead the weak-willed and untrained into wrong paths. A mother's death and the breaking up of family ties, the coming of a harsh stepmother, discord and dissipation in the home,—all these things help to feed disreputable houses.

A well-known social worker gives a pathetic case of a poor girl whose mother died, and whose stepmother would not take her into the home. Though only a mere child, she fell a victim to a white slave trader who treated her with unspeakable cruelty, and she was at last found with a bottle of carbolic acid, on the point of ending her life and the life of her nameless baby.

It IS all very well for people who have plenty to eat and comfortable homes to wonder why girls should have so little stamina and character, and should so easily yield to sin. But when a girl's last dollar is gone and she is weary with hunting for a situation, when hunger stares her in the face, and she is, perhaps, told by her lodging mistress that she "cannot stay on any longer"; when she is thrown out on the street, and there is not one to take a particle of interest in her or to care what becomes of her, how can you, who perhaps do not know what temptation is, be so pitiless to the girl, who, after struggling for a long time, at length goes wrong? She simply enters the only door that opens to her, No other place will take her in; no one else outside of this will give her food and shelter. When we remember that the strongest of us are to a large extent victims of conditions, is it any wonder that a girl in such a distressed mental state goes along the line of least resistance? Then, when a girl is driven to such a place, practically in all cases she looks upon it as only a temporary expedient. She hopes and expects somehow to redeem her mistake before it becomes known. But it is always the old story.♦ It is just like the drunkard who goes through life always expecting to reform. He firmly believes that each debauch will be his last; but he does not realize the iron grip of habit, which fastens tighter and tighter upon him, and that each time he indulges he makes another indulgence more certain.

If, instead of building so many libraries and endowing so many universities, our Carnegies and Rockefellers would build some hotels for women, similar to the Mills hotels for men, what a wonderful boon it would be for thousands of poor girls who come to the cities seeking positions!

Contrast the difference in the great city of New York, for instance, between the provision made for youths by the Young Men's Christian Associations and the enormous Mills hotels, and the pitiable lack of provision for poor, homeless, defenseless girls, who have a thousand more temptations than men and who are not half so able to protect themselves.

Forty or fifty years ago the white slave traffic was practically unknown in this country. The enormous influx of girls and women into the industrial world within this period largely explains its introduction among us. To-day about sixty per cent, of all the young women in America are engaged in various occupations, —and our present economic system is largely responsible for their exploitation for vicious purposes. Commercial greed grinds the souls of defenseless girls and women into dividends and compels them to exist on starvation wages, thus exposing them to all sorts of perils and temptations.

Another chief aid to the white slave traffic has been the almost criminal custom of bringing up girls without protecting their future by making them self-supporting, without fitting them to earn their own living in some practical way.

Parents little realize what a terrible thing it is to let girls grow up without learning a trade or occupation by which they can get an independent living or protect their self-respect and dignity, and then allow them to drift into the city to struggle as best they can for an existence. When comparatively few men, even those who have had special training, are able to get little more than a decent living, and tens of thousands fail to do that, what shall we say of the chances of the tradeless, occupationless, helpless girls who are thrown unprepared into the modern maelstrom of strife and selfish struggle for bread, for place, and for power!

Mothers are often to blame for this. I know some of them who would never even let their daughters harden or redden their soft white hands by washing dishes or doing house-work. They would do the drudgery themselves and let their girls sit around and read silly novels, because they wanted them to have an easier time in life than they had had. Then, when these girls grow up untrained, untaught, unsophisticated, ignorant of themselves, ignorant of the meaning of their sex; when, perhaps, the family meets with reverses, or for some reason or other they are forced to find a means of livelihood, they naturally drift into already overcrowded cities. We should not wonder that so many of them fall into sin, but rather that the majority of them are saved from this terrible fate.

It is imperatively necessary that all parents, whether rich or poor, see that their children, and especially their daughters, learn a trade, or become sufficiently expert in some occupation to enable them to be self-supporting. Even the daughters of wealthy parents are not secure from sudden changes of fortune, and without this safeguard and assurance for her future in this age of specialization and fierce competition a girl may be tremendously tempted to drift into vice.

It ought to be a misdemeanor punishable by law to allow girls to go out into the world to earn a living without all the possible safeguards which a good education, good moral training, and a practical knowledge of some good trade or profession can supply. Where parents are incompetent or unable to furnish these the State should see to it that no girl is obliged to face life without being thus prepared and safeguarded.

"I am no alarmist" is a half-apologetic expression often heard in the speech or seen in the writings of many who deal with this subject, but the writer has no such apology to make. As with "the voice of one crying in the wilderness," he wishes to warn with the greatest emphasis of which words are capable every one under the stress of sexual temptation, but whose feet have not yet slipped or have slipped but little in its dubious and treacherous paths. In dealing with the "white slavery" of the twentieth century, he would, if possible, add fire and force to the ringing words of James

Russell Lowell in dealing with the black slavery of the nineteenth century:

"In God's name let all who hear, nearer and nearer, the hungry moan of the storm and the growl of the breakers, speak out! But, alas, we have no right to interfere. If a man pluck an apple of mine, he shall be in danger of the justice; but, if he steal my brother, I must be silent. Who says this? Our Constitution, consecrated by the callous consuetude of sixty years, and grasped in triumphant argument by the left hand of him whose right hand clutches the clotted slave-whip. Justice, venerable with the undethronable majesty of countless aeons, says,— speak! The Past, wise with the sorrows and desolations of ages, from amid her shattered fanes and wolf-housing palaces, echoes,— speak! Nature, through her thousand trumpets of freedom, her stars, her sunrises, her seas, her winds, her cataracts, her mountains blue with cloudy pines, blows jubilant encouragement, and cries,— speak ! From the soul's trembling abysses the still, small voice not vaguely murmurs,— speak! But alas! the Constitution and the Honorable Mr. Bagowind, M.C., say,— be dumb!"

But far be it from the author to speak or write one word that might add to the woes of those whose feet have thus slipped and who are now suffering the deplorable consequences. Even to the most miserable, the most remorseful, the most despairing of all such victims, "whose eyes fail with wakefulness and tears, and ache for the dark house and the long sleep," he would most earnestly and reverently commend the pitying words of Him of Nazareth, who came to save the lost and who said, "Neither do I condemn thee; go, and sin no more,"—also the words of the Lord of All, as quoted by the prophet Isaiah i, 18, "Though your sins be as scarlet, they shall be white as snow; though they be red like crimson, they shall be as wool."

The night is mother of the day,

The winter of the spring. And ever upon old decay

The greenest mosses cling; Behind the cloud the starlight lurks.

Through showers the sunbeams fall. For God, who loveth all His works,

Has left His hope with all.—J. G. Whittier.

15

PERILS OF THE NEW FREEDOM

«It is the little rift within the lute
That by and by will make the music mute,
And, ever widening, slowly silence all."

"If I had a daughter," said the late Kyrle Bellew to an interviewer, "I wouldn't let her get within speaking distance of a matinee actor, but I'd let her go to the matinee and fall in love with the hero whenever she wanted to. Not with the actor, you know, but with the part he plays; that's the difference, and it's a whole lot of difference, too."

In these words Mr. Bellew showed his intimate knowledge of girl nature, and also his sympathy with its romanticism.

"It's all wrong," he went on, "the way people talk of the matinee girl and her folly. I've seen lots of good, wholesome, clever girls dead in love with a hero,—not with the actor who played him, but with the hero,—and the poor fool of a conceited actor misunderstood the whole affair.

"A little slip of a girl, with her head full of fairy tales, goes to the matinee. She lives at home with a father who reads the paper all the time he's in the house, and her only brother never notices her at all, except to tweak her hair or make fun of all her timid ideas.

"When the hero appears the little girl is electrified. "Here,' she thinks, here's the kind of man I've dreamed of. He fears nothing, he loves with all his heart, he doesn't laugh at the idea of a locket and a ring. Why, he'd die for a lock of his lady's hair.' And she sits and dreams and dreams, dear little goose."

Unfortunately not all actors, nor does the public generally, see the sometimes silly conduct of the matinee girl in its true light. Girls are often severely blamed and criticized for actions and words which are merely the expression of hero worship or romantic idealism. But it is true, too, that there are many girls who overstep the limits of good behavior, and leave themselves open to well-deserved criticism.

The freedom accorded to girls to-day, as compared with the restraints imposed upon their sisters of half or a quarter of a century ago, is often responsible for this. Indeed, it is safe to say that, until she is protected by the knowledge that will save her from the snares and pitfalls of life, the larger liberty the modern girl enjoys is, in many instances, a source of danger. The fact that our girls go out into the world with very little training and few suggestions regarding the risks they run in mingling with men in business life of whom they know practically nothing; the mother's fatal failure to instruct her daughter regarding the possible curse of the first kiss, the first cocktail, or the slightest familiarity has often led to sorrow and shame.

How little the average girl realizes what she is doing when she drinks cocktails with men, even at a respectable hotel or restaurant. The first cocktail, the first kiss, or the first embrace is often the very gateway to perdition.

Not long ago I heard a man reprove a girl companion very sharply because she refused to drink a cocktail. She told him that she thought her mother would not like it, to which the man retorted that, if she ever expected to have a good time in life, she would have to be a "good fellow."

Who can estimate the human tragedies that have resulted from getting such false notions of comradeship as this! Trying to be a "good fellow" has opened the door to ruin for multitudes of young girls.

Many a light-hearted girl without the slightest idea of doing wrong goes motoring with a comparative stranger and does not even hesitate to stop at road houses for refreshments. Or she will attend the theatre without a chaperone and afterwards go to wine suppers, at which she is exposed to all sorts of dangers of which she is totally ignorant.

Most mothers trust their daughters too implicitly even to think they could ever be led astray, no matter what company they are thrown in. It is true that a pure heart and the power of self-control, backed by wise training, will protect any girl under almost any circumstances anywhere in the world. But how many girls are so protected? And how many mothers have any idea of the perils which their daughters are constantly encountering, and what narrow escapes many of them have?

How often do we hear ignorant, well-meaning, girls who have been unfortunately entangled weeping bitter tears of anguish that their mothers never told them of the risks of un-chaperoned association with men!

It is a terrible thing to send girls out into the world, especially the business world, where they come in constant, close contact with men, without posting them in regard to the special temptations and perils they will encounter. Parents might as well expect that lambs would be safe in pastures infested with wolves as to send ignorant, innocent young girls out among men, many of whom are brutal and sensual, and expect them to remain unharmed. If any human being in this world should be pitied, it is an ignorant, unsophisticated girl or young woman exposed to its dangerous temptations.

There is no doubt that the new freedom of girls, with much less of the old-time chaperon-age, the multiplied opportunities and facilities for saying rash things, fool things over the telephone; the great increase in number of places of amusement, such as moving picture shows, the hotel and afternoon teas, where dancing is indulged in, and especially automobile temptations—all these things give girls opportunity to form unfortunate associations. In other words, many of the safeguards formerly thrown around a young woman have been removed, while she has infinitely greater liberties, with far more temptations to go astray.

While this new and larger freedom which girls (who carry their own night key) all over the country are enjoying, and insisting upon, will result in great good to those who have strong characters and who are fortunate enough to have intelligent and helpful mothers, it will lead to infinite harm to the weak daughters of weak mothers, who do not appreciate its dangers.

A New York mother whom I know has been driven almost to insanity by the waywardness of her seventeen-year-old daughter, who, under the pretense of calling on friends, goes alone to hotel teas and cabaret restaurants, where she has formed the acquaintance of questionable men, with whom she dances and goes automobile riding. The girl has become so fascinated with the excitement, and what she calls the fun of her new liberty, that she pays no attention to the warnings of her mother, who doesn't dare to tell the father, a very stern man, lest he should disinherit her. Sometimes this girl does not get home until two or three o'clock in the morning, or remains out all night with her girl chums and then resorts to all sorts of deceptions to keep the truth from her father.

Many girls insist on doing as this one does, going out unattended to all sorts of places. They meet unprincipled men who invite them to the theatre and out riding, often taking them to road houses and inducing them to drink wine and to smoke cigarettes. Cases have been reported during the past year of unfortunate, unsuspecting girls who have been drugged in these places and thus led to their ruin.

Only the other day I heard a beautiful young woman speak of girl friends who, even though they were chaperoned at balls and dances, would take occasion when they were not observed to slip away with young men partners, and go out motoring, perhaps for an hour or two, without being missed or exciting the suspicion of their chaperones.

Now, this is adding deceit to imprudence, and it will not be long before girls who indulge in escapades of this kind will be drawn into others far more serious and more dangerous.

One would think that the frightful experiences of girls like Nan Patterson, the Florodora chorus girl, would be warning enough for hundreds of others who are trying to see how near they can go to the edge of the precipice without falling over.

The allurements of a gay life, the passion for admiration, the love of extravagance and show, not the love of wrongdoing, led to the ruin of this unfortunate girl, as it is leading to that of thousands of others.

It does not seem possible for any intelligent girl to go on doing dangerous things, attending champagne-stage suppers, motoring at night with men whom she barely knows, and exposing herself to' unspeakable risks without realizing where it will all end. But it is a curious fact that, when people are in the midst of a whirl of dissipation, they are blind to the results, they cannot see what others see, what others know will be the inevitable outcome. The actors in the game seem to be hypnotized. They know what has been the result of the pace they are going with thousands of others, but they do not believe it is going to be the same with them. It is the old story of the young man who drinks. He thinks that he can stop drinking any time, can reform when he pleases, but everybody else knows that he is being grasped more and more firmly in the clutches of the tyrant habit, and that every day that goes by makes it less and less probable that he will ever escape from them. There is something about the light and glare, the lure of dissipation, which not only makes one blind to all its dangers, but also hides from him the havoc that it is playing in his life.

Another danger of the new girl's greater freedom is that it tends to make her too independent of other people's opinions. She is apt to think that she is just as free as her brother, and can do the same things that he does with the same impunity, which is practically not the case.

It may be a false standard of ethics, but it is unfortunately true that, if a girl is indiscreet and happens to make a mistake, if she appears at some questionable place, no matter how innocent she may be of wrongdoing, if she is seen with a man who has a bad reputation, she is quickly gossiped about and her character assailed.

Again, many girls call up men over the telephone during business hours and talk to them as freely as their brothers talk to their men friends. After a while they acquire the telephone habit, the habit of calling up male acquaintances and saying things to them just because they are at a distance which they would not think of saying in a letter or if they were speaking face to face. We all have more or less what we might call long-distance courage; it is so easy to say things over the telephone, when one is far away, which modesty and sensitiveness would restrain one from saying at close range. While the telephone has proved an untold blessing to millions, it has been the undoing of a great many modest, good-intentioned girls; and this is especially true of girls who were brought up in very strict homes, where the parents would not allow them any liberties, nor tell them why they considered it necessary to be so strict in their surveillance.

Most girls know that they should not do indiscreet things, but they do not begin to know how fatally, how tragically wrong these things may be. Heedless of public opinion in doing foolish or imprudent things, many of them say that they don't care what people think or say of them. "She did not care what people said," would make a fitting epitaph for many a girl who has gone wrong. It is not always enough to be conscious that we are innocent; not enough to know that we do what is right; we must not put ourselves in questionable positions. Girls should avoid the appearance of evil, avoid questionable situations, avoid the company of men of known bad character. Nor should they carry on silly conversations over the telephone with men whom they barely know.

A girl who doesn't care what people say about her, does not realize that gossip has a multitude of tongues, and that bad things said about people are infinitely more contagious than good things. She does not realize how much her welfare, her success in life depends upon what people think of her. No one is independent of the opinion of others any more than a drop of water in the ocean is independent of the other drops. Even the appearance of evil should be shunned.

16
WOMAN'S CRUELTY TO WOMAN

Charity is the brightest star in the Christian's diadem.

Don't look for the flaws as you go through life.

And, even when you find them. It's wise and kind to be somewhat blind

And look for the virtues behind there.

— Ella Wheeler Wilcox.

But still believe that story wrong Which ought not to be true.— SHERIDAN.

Then gently scan your brother man.

Still gentler sister woman; Though they may gang a trifle wrang,

To step aside is human: One point must still be greatly dark,

The moving why they do it; And just as lamely can ye mark

How far, perhaps, they rue it. — Robert Burns.

In a recent investigation by the Woman's and Child's Wage Earning Association, it was found that a majority of the girls who go wrong come from the domestic service. The chief reasons assigned for this were long hours, the monotony of the work, dark, gloomy sleeping rooms, and no place in which to receive company.

The report will come as a great surprise to many, especially to the employers of domestic servants and to those who are fond of painting in glowing colors the sheltered, fortunate, and, on the whole, happy life of the average girl who does housework.

When shop or factory girls complain of low wages and long hours, they are asked, by those who take this roseate view of the life of house servants, why they don't give up their wearisome, ill paid toil and work in a family where they will be well fed, well housed, and well paid; in short, where they will have the comforts of a good home, with no temptations to draw them from the straight and narrow path.

If these good people who think the lives of domestic servants are so desirable could only take their places, for a week or two, they would, in all probability, revise their opinion. If the average house mistress only realized how utterly dependent upon her are her servants for their social life, their opportunities for recreation, for development, for anything that is bright and cheerful in their lives, her attitude toward them might be very different.

I would not imply that all mistresses are indifferent to, and have no thought or care for, the welfare and happiness of their servants. Nor would I suggest that all servants are unhappy and discontented. Far from it. There are some kind and thoughtful mistresses, some happy and contented maids. But, without entering upon a discussion of the much debated servant question, the report of the investigation committee of the Woman's and Child's Wage Earning Association would certainly indicate that thoughtless mistresses and discontented maids are in the majority.

Can we wonder, when we stop to think how little encouragement, inspiration or appreciation the average domestic servant gets out of her work, which is usually dreary, monotonous drudgery?

The pathetic side of the whole servant problem, which has been before the public so long, is that the girls in domestic work are shut out, practically, from human relationship. They have little or no opportunity for social intercourse, for clean companionship with the opposite sex. They meet their male acquaintances or friends under unfavorable, often dangerous conditions. The very lack of a proper place to receive friends or callers makes their social life abnormal.

How would you feel, you mistresses, who are often so hard and unsympathetic with your servants, if your own daughter had to receive her men friends in a dingy kitchen, with nothing but hard, wooden chairs to sit on, and perhaps not enough of these? Suppose she was not even allowed to receive callers in the kitchen, and could only stand out in the alleyway or go with them to a public park, or meet them in cheap dance halls! Would you not be unhappy and miserable about her? You forget that your servant girls have just the same longing for affection, the same yearning for a home of their own, the same desire for social intercourse as your daughter.

Kipling says: "The Colonel's lady and Judy O'Grady are sisters under their skin." Whether in a palace or a hovel, in the breast of a fine lady or that of a poor working girl, the human heart has the same craving, the same desire for love, companionship. The human mind, without distinction of class or race, is so constituted that it must have variety; our passions, longings and desires all clamor for expression, and if they are denied, there is starvation going on in the nature. How can you expect your servants to be normal when their whole life is one-sided; when many sides of their nature, those which you are constantly developing and feeding in yourself, are practically never appealed to in them? Their pent-up desires, their yearnings, whatever they may be, are unexpressed, and these feelings are dangerous when thus repressed, for they will seek an outlet in other directions, often in forbidden ways.

Mrs. Mary Hutton Pell, recognizing the importance of this seldom considered phase of the question, has solved it entirely to her own satisfaction and that of her servants. In a recent interview on the subject she said, "People are all the time wailing about the servant problem, but they never try to solve the question. Nothing has ever been done for the domestic servant. Workers in all other hues have been helped in various ways; the shop girl, the factory workers have amusements provided for them, different kinds of welfare work have been organized for them, but there is never anything for the domestic servant. Instead of helping the servants, we degrade them.— There is no other class of workers whose general condition has such an important bearing upon family life, and there are no other workers so little known. We never think of doing anything for their amusement or seeing that they have any diversion."

Another progressive woman, Mrs. Ellen Trask, says: "It is not so much the maids who need training as the mistresses. Women have for so long a time kept their housemaids in a state of semi-bondage that they cannot seem to realize that it may be possible to alter the conditions in some way that will give satisfaction to both.

"It is easy to train young girls to be good housekeepers. It is the natural work of women, and many of them love it. But, so long as girls are expected to be inmates night and day of some other woman's home, no matter how luxurious it may be or how well they may be treated, the problem will remain a problem.

""Is there any other work where the employee is expected to be under the constant supervision of her employer? If only someone can devise a way to bring the two into more equable relations with each other, there will be hope of solving the problem.

"We don't need to have ignorant girls fresh from a foreign country in our homes. We can have intelligent girls, trained in our own schools, if we make the conditions right for them. Shall we continue in the old way, or shall we use the same intelligence which is used in the suffrage problem and find the remedy?"

One of the chief troubles in this whole question is that the average mistress forgets, in dealing with her maids, that "man does not live by bread alone," and that even where the material conditions are all right there is a human, a social side to the girls who work in her home that clamors for recognition, for expression. While society is pushing onward in every other direction, and education is lifting the humble and lowly born to positions of honor and great responsibility, this side of the servant problem remains where it was. There is no hopeful outlook, no chance of advancement in the life of the house worker, and women cannot shirk responsibility for this. They are largely to blame, and, until they recognize the social rights of the domestic class, their equality, at least on broad human lines, with themselves, the servant problem will remain unsolved. Mistresses must also take their share of responsibility for the fall of so many girls in this class.

What are the chances, for example, that a really intelligent servant girl, who, perhaps has come out of a good home in the country, will, under the conditions of her new life in the average city home, meet a man whom she would care to marry? Her very situation prejudices the men who are her equals. Her very lack of opportunity probably bars her from making a suitable marriage. She realizes this, and it is especially brought home to her when she feels that she is getting along in years; that, perhaps, her attractiveness is being burned up over the cook stove and wasted over the washtub; and that she is growing prematurely old because her girlhood is being crushed out from lack of recreation, from the unvarying monotony of her long daily routine. • Is it strange that girls thus circumstanced grasp even at the counterfeit of love, that which comes nearer than anything else in their lives to resembling the real affection which they crave? They drift from their cold, dark, ugly quarters to where there is at least life and activity. Though degrading, there is something human in it for which their natures are starving. They do not yet know all its awful wretchedness. They have not yet drunk the bitterest dregs from their cup.

"Man's inhumanity to man makes countless thousands mourn," says Burns; but what of woman's inhumanity to woman?

Woman's cruelty to woman is responsible for a great many domestic servants drifting into disreputable houses. Women generally have accepted the double standard established by man, with its exoneration of the male wrongdoer and ostracism of the woman.

Someone has said that "no one else can be so hard as a good woman," and in the case of a fallen sister this is, alas! too often true. I have heard good women condemn in the harshest and bitterest terms young girls who were led astray in the first instance by men old enough to be their fathers, in some instances, their grandfathers, with never a word of blame for the men.

When a husband, a son, or a brother goes wrong, where does the wife, the mother, or the sister place the blame ? Is it not invariably on "the other woman," that "horrid" other woman who tempted the poor, helpless innocent man! How could a grandfather, or father, protect himself from the wiles of that young Delilah? It was she who tempted him, and he did, like Adam, "eat of the forbidden fruit." No matter if Delilah be but fifteen, and Samson be fifty, no matter if his long experience in hypnotizing innocent girls (whose mothers had never posted them regarding their own sex nature) placed the young girl at a criminal disadvantage, it is she who should have known better, she who should have been able to withstand temptation, she who should have shown herself of the stronger sex, not of the weaker. Her passions? Why, she has none,—or, at least, according to man's theory regarding her,— which women have meekly accepted,—she should have none. It is the man only who has passions to fight, temptations to conquer. The woman is simply weak and vicious; she acts out of pure wantonness!

Women have certainly learned well the lesson that has been taught them for centuries, that began with our father Adam, when, after enjoying his apple, he tried to shield himself from the anger of his Lord by putting all the blame for their joint disobedience on our poor Mother Eve,—"The woman did tempt me and I did eat!"

So when a woman discovers that a servant has been betrayed by her lover (often because she had no decent place in which to receive her male friends), instead of protecting the girl, trying to help her out of a trouble which she feels will ruin her life, instead of trying to shield her by getting a place for her in the country or in a hospital, she turns her out with abusive language, telling her that she is unfit to associate with human beings.

If there is ever a time when a girl who is alone in the world, whose very longing for affection, for someone to love her, has, perhaps, led her into trouble, needs the sympathy, the protection, the shielding which her mistress could give her, it is when she is in this condition.

Is it any wonder that so many of these frightened, friendless girls, who dare not whisper their trouble to any human being, commit suicide, or that they become objects of public charity, or, when they leave the hospital, drift through the only door that seems open to them ?

Frank Moss, Assistant District Attorney of New York, tells a pathetic story of a German girl who was living with Wolter, the degenerate murderer of Ruth Wheeler, the fifteen-year-old girl whom he lured to his rooms by an advertisement for a stenographer. When summoned as a witness in the murder trial, this German girl, in answer to the question whether she loved Wolter, said "Yes." "Then you will probably not tell the truth about him," said Mr. Moss. "The truth?" she cried. "I must tell the truth whatsoever the results," and she did.

After the trial Mr. Moss said he was so affected by the girl's honesty and pitied her so in her awful plight that he asked her if she could not go to friends or relatives when she had testified and was released from the House of Detention. "No, Mr. Moss," replied the girl, "I have not a friend in America who would shield me or do anything for me." The kind-hearted lawyer involuntarily kissed her hand, and told her "You have one friend left." He, with others, assisted her to get a position, and every little while she reported at his office.

After a few months she came to him one day with her little son in her arms, accompanied by a big, robust German, who said he wanted to marry her. Mr. Moss asked the man if he knew her history. He said he did, but that he loved her and wanted to make her his wife. The pair were married, and the District Attorney, with Mr. Moss and all the other assistant attorneys, attended the wedding. A short time after the husband came to the District Attorney's office and told him that he wanted legally to adopt his wife's boy, to educate him, and bring him up right.

Tens of thousands of girls could be rescued as this German girl was if they only had a little friendly sympathy and the aid of good people. But they are cruelly and almost criminally treated as outcasts by the very people who could help them.

It is doubtful if any normal girl ever goes willingly into a vicious life with the least idea of remaining in it. But, unfortunately, when girls once get into it, they very rarely leave it. A sense of shame and the gradual loss of self-respect undermine their will power; and, when they realize that it would be almost impossible to face the world again, when almost everybody shuns, scorns and denounces the girl who has made a mistake, they give themselves up for lost.

The totally wrong view society takes of this whole question is responsible for thousands of girls remaining in an evil life when they long to get away from their horrible experiences. They know how they would be despised by society; that there would be no chance for them again in the world outside; and they think all they can do is to continue to live in the underworld and to get as much out of their wretched life as possible. People outside know nothing of the terrible suffering of these girls, the torturing existence they lead, especially during the first months of their debauchery. Every day, until their self-respect has died out of them, many of them cry their hearts out for the sight, the caress of loved ones whom they will never see again.

Happily there are signs of a widespread awakening in regard to this whole question of sexual immorality. The tendency is to be more merciful to the woman who has gone wrong and to put the chief blame where, in most cases, it belongs, on the man. While the conservative, the narrow-minded and the ignorant still cling to the prescribed masculine ethics of the double standard, with its blind injustice and immorality, progressive women, women of education and intelligence, are being aroused to a sense of the iniquity of the traditional attitude toward the fallen woman. They are taking, rather, the attitude of Elizabeth Fry in her work among the women in English prisons a century ago. These unfortunates worshipped that noble Quaker lady, and a friend visiting Newgate one day in company with her, being struck by the affectionate manner of the prisoners toward her, inquired for what crimes the women had been convicted. "I do not know," was the reply. "I have never asked them that. We all have come short."

Women's clubs, Social Settlements, Rescue Homes, the Salvation Army, and great bodies of Church workers all over the country are doing an immense amount of good in rescuing women and girls from lives of shame and putting them in positions where they will be self-supporting and free from temptations.

At a recent meeting of clubwomen, members of the Salvation Army and other social workers in New York, to establish additional facilities for rescue work, Mrs. Robbins Lau remarked, "Men have said that woman's worst enemy is woman. It is possible that this rebuke was merited in the past, but I believe the clubwomen of New York are now making an honest effort to remove the cause of the reproach."

Mrs. William Grant Brown, another well-known clubwoman who spoke at the meeting, said: "At some remote period men may be depended upon absolutely to respect the purity of women, but until that time arrives we must try to do something to repair the injury done through the wickedness of men and the frailty of their victims."

But it was Brigadier Brown, of the Salvation Army, who touched the most vital part of the matter, and, even at the risk of unduly dwelling on this phase of the question, I cannot forbear quoting her in part. "The most aggravating problem which confronts us in this work," she said, "is how to keep our daughters safe after they have been rescued. You know the world is very cruel. It is cruel without intending to be so. In its indifference it often inflicts mortal wounds, and the girl who has endured struggles and gone through trials which are known only to her class often succumbs.

"In sickness she has nowhere to go, and when thrown out of employment she is at a greater disadvantage than is she who has never violently fractured the moral law.

"Of course the Salvation Army does not believe in coddling or nursing the unfortunate or the wrongdoer. We peremptorily insist on everybody working. We believe work is absolutely necessary to the construction and preservation of a morally healthy as well as a physically healthy citizenship. But how nice it would be for a girl who has taken a wayward step to be assured that she has a heart and a home to come to in case of dire need!"

Too much cannot be said in praise of the rescue work that is being done by many devoted women all over the country. But our great aim must be total abolition of sexual vice, —the prevention of immorality rather than healing its ravages.

Employers can do a great deal to stem the tide of immorality which statisticians have found in the domestic field. There is a movement on foot for the rehabilitation and uplift of the workers in this most conservative and tradition-bound of all fields of employment. Mistresses on the one hand, and maids on the other, are forming organizations for a general campaign of betterment. More and better education along scientific lines for the maids; more consideration, and better provision for their social needs on the part of the mistresses, is the slogan of this movement. We need better educated, better trained women in this most important branch of social service. We shall get them when the relations of mistress and maid, or rather employer and employee, are on a different basis, and the hours of work are regulated and systematized as they are in all other legitimate businesses. Then the social stigma that attaches to domestic work will be removed, and the domestic employee will take her proper place as one of the most useful and important of all public or private servants.

Who made the heart, 'tis He alone

Decidedly can try us, He knows each chord,—its various tone,

Each spring,—its various bias: Then at the balance let's be mute.

We never can adjust it; What's dons we partly may compute.

But know not what's resisted. — Robert Burns.

17

THE DAMNABLE DOUBLE STANDARD

There is no sex in morals.

Whatever is morally right for a man to do is morally right for a woman to do; I recognize no rights but human rights.

— Angelina Grimke Weld.

Recently, we are told, a woman standing high in the social circles of her city crossed off the names of two young men from her invitation list. The action was bound to be noticed, and it was. Several friends went to her and pleaded for the young men. "Of course it is unfortunate," they argued, "that they are not just what they should be, but you are very likely to drive them farther toward ruin by your action in so publicly calling attention to their habits by excluding them from your social affairs." The social leader listened. "No," she said, firmly, "you are wrong. We have all been wrong in opening the doors of our houses to them. I warned both of them that I would do this if they did not mend their ways; and, while they listened respectfully, they went right on. For the sake of my own two daughters, and the daughters of other mothers who come to my house, my doors are closed to them." The woman's stand had the effect of helping more timid and wavering mothers, and before the season was over practically every door was closed to the young men.

If all women would unite in taking the stand adopted by this social leader toward male sexual sinners, the most damnable feature of our civilization, the double standard of morals, which makes a woman an outcast for the immorality which is overlooked in a man, would soon be a thing of the past.

It seems almost incredible that this vilely unjust standard should have endured so long; that, in Christian countries, among the followers of that Christ who so clearly condemned it, a man should be socially ostracized for comparatively minor criminal offences, yet be rotten with sexual immorality and still have access to the best homes; while a woman who makes the least false step in this direction should become a pariah.

Is there any colorable pretext for such a distinction? Are the effects of impurity in a man less disastrous than in a woman? Is there any sex in principle? Is there any reason why a man should have license to drag himself through licentious mire any more than a woman? A thousand times, no! It would be loosening the very foundations of virtue to countenance the notion that, because of the difference in sex, men are at liberty to set morality at defiance and to do with impunity that which, if done by women, would stain the latter's character and make them outcasts forever. All right-minded people must agree with Angelina Grimke Weld that "whatever is morally right for a man to do is morally right for a woman to do; I recognize no rights but human rights."

It is because human rights have been ignored in the past, because one sex has arrogated all rights, all power, to itself, and dominated the other sex, that we have the absurd and monstrous paradox of a double standard of morals.

In the past, human society has been man-made, with the exception of a little dash here and there of the feminine which woman has been allowed to slip in because it favored man's own pleasures. Because they have had the power, men have always made a great distinction between male and female sex offenders. They have always sought security for their own moral lapses. They are responsible for the wicked difference in public opinion regarding the sins of the two sexes,—for the unjust sex distinction which has encouraged and promoted immorality and given license to vice through all the centuries.

Discussing the status of woman in China and its underlying causes, Prof. E. A. Ross, in his remarkable book, "The Changing Chinese," might be quoted almost literally in describing the causes responsible for the double standard of morals, with all its attendant evils, in Christian countries.

"Balancing their burdens against those of the men, it is clear that the laws governing woman's life are not for the sake of society or the race so much as for the male sex. In its every chapter Chinese culture is man-made and betrays the native male viewpoint. Although necessary, woman is inferior and must be held under firm control. The sages stressed the danger of letting women become educated and go about freely, for thus might women gain the upper hand and wreck society.

"From the male viewpoint it is fitting that woman be sacrificed to man, but not that man be sacrificed to woman. . . .

"The wife guilty of unfaithfulness is to be stoned, drowned, or hanged. ... If a husband be found unfaithful, his wife has a right to scold him good and hard, and he ought not to beat her for it, either.

"Nothing could be plainer than that woman's lot in China is not of her own fashioning, but has been shaped by male tastes and prejudices, without regard to what women themselves think about it. The men have determined woman's sphere as well as man's. The ancient sages—all men,—molded the institutions that bear upon women, and it is male comment, not really public opinion, that enforces the conventionalities that crush her. By wit, will, or worth, the individual woman may slip from under the thumb of the individual man,—there are many such cases,—but never could the sex free itself from the domination of the male sex. The men had all the artillery,—the time-hallowed teachings and institutions,—and all the small arms,—current opinion and comment. Cribbed and confined, the women were without schooling, locomotion, acquaintance, conversation, stimulus, contact with affairs, access to ideas, or opportunity to work out their own point of view."

But even in the tradition-bound Orient, as well as throughout Christendom, the women are rebelling against man-made laws; they are demanding that they be governed by the same civil and moral codes that apply to men. They are insisting on a higher, cleaner, purer standard of society than that which obtained in the past, a standard to which men shall measure up as well as women, or be ostracized, even as women have been ostracized for not living up to the standard established for them by men.

The leaven of the feminine ideal, which is slowly gaining admission into the life of the world, is already working a mighty revolution in society. Woman's activities in the modern world are hastening the evolution of the race to higher levels.

There was a time when polygamy was not only universal but was also respected. We read in Holy Writ that the wise King Solomon had a thousand wives. All through the Old Testament references are made to the numerous wives of men. Many things were allowed in the early history of the race which would not be tolerated to-day. More and more, as woman climbs to her rightful place, that assigned her at the beginning by the Creator, does man tend to become a higher and nobler being.

A century ago the mistresses of kings and emperors ruled the courts of the world. Rulers carried on their amours openly, in defiance of all the ideals of morality or decency. High government officials were obliged to recognize their favorites and bow to their tremendous social and political power.

The rulers of to-day must at least preserve the appearance of morality. They must cover up their intrigues, hide them from the world, thus showing a little respect for public opinion and an improvement in the ideal of masculine morals. A hundred years ago men in general led immoral lives much more openly than at present. These things are more and more covered and carried on in secret, showing the growing change in society's view not only of sexual immorality but also of all other forms of vice. Men are being forced to clean up their lives in every direction. Compare, for example, the drinking habits of men in public life to-day with those of the corresponding classes of. a hundred years ago. It was a common thing for great lawyers of that time to be so drunk at important trials that they would scarcely know what they were doing. Urgent cases would sometimes have to be postponed until the legal lights had recovered from their debauches. It was the usual thing for liquors to be kept in stores and all sorts of places of business for employers and employees. Clergymen, deacons and other officials of the church often drank to excess. At public dinners and on other public occasions it was not unusual for men to drink until they fell under the table, and the man who could drink the most men under the table was looked up to by the others as a superior man.

It is not necessary to go back even so far to accentuate the marked change in social standards. It is not very long since our public men would brag about the large number of their illicit sex relations and boast of debauching innocent girls. Gambling was universal, and it was a common thing for members of our national congress and senate to stagger to their seats. They would often have to be removed in a state of beastly intoxication.

For centuries the sowing of wild oats by youths and young men was considered justifiable, even necessary for a well-poised, virile youth. It was thought that every boy who was going to make a real man "must have his fling." Indeed, because of the beastliness of men in the earlier history of the race for ages, the mutual loyalty of men and women was thought practically impossible. But, as the race rises higher in the scale of civilization, these ideals and practices are passing away and higher and purer standards of morals and conduct are taking their place.

"There was a long era when the separate standard of morals for the two sexes was accepted by all good people," says Ella Wheeler Wilcox. " "Boys will be boys' was the extreme of criticism passed on a fallen boy, but any girl who lost her reputation was shunned and shut from all respectable circles save the back pews of a church, where she must go veiled, and the only doors open to her were those of the convent, the Magdalene Home, or the tomb. But the world has changed mightily-"

Yes, the world has changed wonderfully, it is true; but the double standard, being the strongest and most firmly entrenched of man-made social canons, is, naturally, one of the most difficult to displace; and, as it is the one that has wrought most evil in society, so its complete abolition will do more to lift mankind to a higher plane than any other social reform.

The evils of this double standard—which should be properly called a code of morality for women and of immorality for men,—have hitherto been carefully concealed from those whom they most injured, but the great feminine movement, the awakening of woman, the revelations of sociologists,—all these are bringing them to light, and light is death to all evil. In her remarkable book, "Plain Facts About a Great Evil," Miss Christabel Pankhurst has turned such a flood of illumination on this the greatest of all social evils, that there can no longer be any excuse for ignoring it or trying to cover it up.

The intelligent, progressive women of the world are rising up in protest against the insult it perpetually offers to their womanhood. They are demanding that the social cancer be cured or cut out. They will no longer shut their eyes to the existence of wickedness because it is practised in secrecy. It must be abolished. The chief thing that troubled the immoral man in the past was that his immorality should be found out. Women are no longer satisfied with the covering up of evil. They are going to insist that it be rooted out, that men shall be morally clean. Every intelligent, virtuous girl is going to demand that the man who goes to the altar with her shall go there as clean as he demands that she shall go; and, if he doesn't, she will not go.. If he goes at all, he will have to go with a woman of his own class; one with whom he has secretly consorted but whom he has openly despised. In the future it is going to be impossible for an impure man to marry on a moral plane infinitely above his own, as he has done in the past.

It is also going to be impossible for him to rob a woman of that which is more precious to her than life itself, and then cast her off as a child discards a broken toy without any fear of being called to account by society. The man who would think it a disgrace not to pay a gambling debt, or a debt of "honor," so-called, but would not hesitate for a moment to abandon a poor girl whom he had ruined and who would not feel the slightest sense of responsibility for the unfortunate child he had brought into life and branded with illegitimacy—this sort of man will not be known in the future.

Hitherto boys have been brought up to think that they can do with impunity things that it would be unthinkable for their sisters to do. The idea of the inferiority of women has been so strongly imprinted on their consciousness that it has utterly confused in their minds the distinction between right and wrong in matters of sex.

I know a boy who treats his sisters as if they were nobodies, and is constantly taunting them with his superiority, reminding them that they are girls and that they are not supposed to have the same rights and privileges as men. "Don't you know that girls can't do this sort of thing?" is a favorite expression of his to his sisters. He not only has a certain scorn for them, but even for his mother, because his father has always treated the women of his family as if they were inferior beings. The boy defers to his father and to older men in everything, but he has little respect for women, especially when it comes to a question of opinion or judgment on important matters.

Boys and girls in the majority of families have become so accustomed to the expressions, —"Oh, he is a boy, and you know boys must have their liberty; they can't be sissies," and "Oh, she is a girl, and she must be infinitely more careful than boys. She cannot do this and she cannot do that, because she is a girl,"— that they have come to draw a sharp distinction between the moral standards of the sexes. They have come to think that men can do many things without blame which it would be sinful and wicked for girls to do. They see that boys can drink and indulge in all other sorts of immorality and still maintain a good standing in society, while girls who should dare to do such things would be condemned, despised and banished from the society of all pure, decent people.

This pernicious distinction in the moral training of youth is responsible for the unfortunate impression among the young men of to-day that, even if they have sown their wild oats, even if they have been guilty of all sorts of indiscretions, they can come to the marriage altar without any compunction or remorse for their sins, for the broken laws of • chastity, which they expect their chosen life partner to have kept inviolate.

This one-sided training is entirely due to man-made social laws, to man's views of the sex question, which have always been colored by his own interests, his own selfish, brutal desires. In his assumption of superiority he has demanded absolute purity in the woman he has married, while he has considered it all right to give his polluted self in exchange for the untarnished chastity of his bride.

The vicious double standard prevents many men from marrying, not because they think they are unfit, but because bachelorhood allows them greater license.

Among the thousands of young men in our cities who, financially, are in splendid position to marry, there are many who do not hesitate to say that they do not need to, because they have more freedom and can get more out of life by remaining single.

Not long ago I asked one of this class, a young man with a very fair income and a splendid outlook, why he did not marry and have a home of his own. "Well," he replied, "it doesn't really pay; and, after all, what is there in it for me ? In New York a man can always get a girl when he wants one, and he doesn't have to bother with her when he doesn't want her!"

He added that, if he wished to go to Europe, he could pack his trunk at night and take the steamer the next morning without anyone to object, or anyone to consult; and that he could live in a bachelor apartment, have his valet to take care of him, eat in the best hotels or restaurants, have a good time whenever and wherever he wanted, and be free from all responsibility of wife or children.

In many cases the utter selfishness of such men, their manner of living, their immoral practices, have disqualified them for ever being really in love with women. They have so long violated, outraged, and debauched that sacred sentiment, the love instinct, that they have become immune to it. Their only desire in regard to women is the gratification of their animal instincts, and they know that, whether married or single, society in general will wink at their immoral practices.

But the day is fast coming when the same treatment that is accorded immoral women will be meted out to immoral men.

A new ideal of the coming man, the coming woman, is being formed in the public mind today. A new vista regarding the possibilities of the child is opening out to humanity. In the coming time we shall have no sowers of wild oats, and no reapers, because the double standard of morals will not be tolerated.

The new woman is going to guard the very gates of life as has never been done in the past. She is not going to be satisfied to take a life partner without at least as much physical examination as is required in taking out a life insurance policy, or as is demanded by the government in recruiting soldiers and sailors for the army and navy. The new woman will cut off from her visiting list all double-standard men, the sort of men who to-day live dual lives, who habitually wallow in moral filth, yet are received in good society and are allowed even by mothers to associate with their pure, innocent daughters.

The great scientist, Alfred Russell Wallace, in his recent book, "Social Environment and Moral Progress," predicts that the position of woman in the not distant future will be far higher and more important than any she has ever occupied in the past. He says that in the future "she will be placed in a position of responsibility and power which will render her man's superior, since the future welfare and progress of the race will so largely depend upon her free choice in marriage."

This will be one of the main results of the new and higher morality which will accrue from the abolition of the double standard. This in turn will be greatly accelerated by the new economic independence of woman. As time goes on and she gains more and more financial independence, it will allow her that freedom of choice in marriage which she has never had before. This freedom of choice will be strengthened and enhanced by the fact that, with every new increase of those qualities which go to make a higher race, the terrible excess of male deaths in boyhood and early manhood will gradually disappear, and, instead of the present majority of women in the world, we shall have a majority of men. This will lead to a greater rivalry for wives, and will give to woman the power to reject all the lower types of character for the superbest types.

This does not by any means imply that woman is going to supplant man or usurp his rights. It simply means that she is going to come into her own; that, instead of walking behind man, in his shadow, as in the past, she is going to pull an even yoke, to walk by his side, so that in the future our human government, the whole machinery of justice, and our social institutions, will have that wholeness and completeness, that high standard which can only come through the equal cooperation of the sexes.

The movement for woman suffrage is only one phase of the mighty revolution which is going on in the woman's world. The vote door which is now gradually but surely swinging open to her in many lands is only one of many doors which are already ajar, and through which she will soon pass, bringing the race with her to a higher plane of morals, manners, and living.

The liquor interests and those that profit by vice and immorality of every sort are opposed to woman's suffrage, because they know that, when women everywhere are granted the power of the ballot, their power to make commercial profit by pandering to men's baser passions will be in jeopardy.

One of the secrets of the Englishman's bitter protest against woman's suffrage lies in the sex question. When women get the vote in England, as elsewhere, they will wipe from the statute books the laws that so shamefully discriminate against their sex, in all questions of sexual morality, in favor of men. The age-old question of man, "The woman thou gavest me she has sinned. What shall I do with her?" will then be changed. Neither morality nor justice will be sex-labeled.

When women are enfranchised, they will not long tolerate the heinous injustice of one code of morals for women and another and far different for men. A man's public life, a successful professional or business career, will not always be a cloak for covering a wretched private character. The double standard will go when woman has an equal voice with man in framing legislation. She will then have infinitely more influence in the forming of social conditions. Women of the future will not permit their sisters to be exploited and outraged to feed the low passions of men. When women get the ballot, they will not permit men to hire youths openly to debase and ruin young girls. They will not tolerate conditions that are likely to transmit the poisons of loathsome diseases to unborn children to handicap them for life with deformities or mental deficiencies.

It is woman's very instinct to protect the home, the children, and she knows that saloons and disreputable houses are the worst enemies of the home. She knows that they threaten the very virtues and hazard the success of her children, and who can doubt that she will fight for the well-being of those for whom she has risked her life? Woman has been an uplifting influence in every situation of life, and it is only natural that she should be the same in politics, a field from which she has been arbitrarily shut out by the selfishness and meanness of men, who flatter her by calling her their superior, telling her she is an angel, and then insult her by denying her the very rights they claim for themselves!

It is a strange thing that man, who has ever vaunted himself as the great chivalrous protector of woman, should be so cruel to her in framing laws against her and in making public sentiment in favor of himself and against her in all sex matters.

This is the great trouble with society to-day. The laws are man-made. They are pointed towards man, fitted for him; and they are enforced or not, just in proportion as they affect man's desires. Man alone will not enforce the law which he himself wants to break, but any woman will insist upon penalizing that which she knows debauches her husband and menaces perpetually her children and her home. Wherever woman has dominated, she has refined, elevated, and purified. She has made the home the purest, sweetest place on earth; and, when she gets the power, she will certainly insist on a clean and equal standard of public as well as private morals.

In Norway, where women have the full parliamentary vote, a long delayed measure of justice has been accorded the unmarried mother and her child. Every illegitimate child is insured the right to its father's name and property, and the mother is also provided for. Compare this with the usual situation in countries where men alone make the laws, where the unmarried mother and her child are outside the pale of the law.

While I write, the males of Great Britain including the Government, the Established Church and the Press are gravely discussing the question of "forgiving" the unmarried mothers of "war babies," for their lapse from virtue, but not a word do we hear about "forgiving" the fathers. Oh, no, as usual in such matters there is nothing to be forgiven them because they are men. But the women of England are raising their voices and protests as never before, and through their efforts, if full responsibility is not brought home to the fathers of the unfortunate babies, it is to be hoped that at least some measure of justice will be secured for the mothers. In our country, wherever women have succeeded in winning political rights, the age of consent has been raised to eighteen years; whereas, in most places, where men alone make laws, it is still between fourteen and sixteen.

In the past, having had all the power in their own hands, men have always stood by one another in covering up their moral turpitude, and in being lenient to their vices.' Furthermore, male physicians have carefully kept the secrets and shielded the reputation of immoral men, even when their sins have wrecked their homes, made invalids of their wives, and cursed their children for life.

Man's ideal has dominated society in the past. Woman's is now coming to the front. On every hand, in spite of much sensational talking and writing to the contrary, there are indications of an upward trend. The universal movement for the enfranchisement of women, equal education for both sexes, the entrance of women into the so-called learned professions and especially the steady increase in

Printed in Great Britain
by Amazon